Ink

Presented to

by

on

Message

Ink

DISCOVER THE POWER OF THE PEN IN A DIGITAL WORLD

ROD GRAY

Ink

DISCOVER THE POWER OF THE PEN IN A DIGITAL WORLD

Published by JMMT GROUP LLC | Cypress, Texas

ISBN (Paperback): 979-8-9992245-0-7

ISBN (Hardback): 979-8-9992245-1-4

ISBN (EPub): 979-8-9992245-2-1

Library of Congress Control Number (LCCN): 2025912397

Printed in the United States of America

Share your stories, schedule speaking engagements, and connect with Rod Gray.

WEBSITE: inkpowerofthepen.com

EMAIL: rod@inkpowerofthepen.com

SOCIAL MEDIA:

FACEBOOK: Rod Gray

INSTAGRAM: @rodgray00

X (FORMERLY TWITTER): @rodgray

LINKEDIN: Rod Gray

Praise for Ink

Rod structures the story of the 'why' we need the handwritten note in a style that invites his readers to be inspired through history and emotional examples. This book will help you get back to the basics.

TRIP DURHAM
2D Consulting, LLC | NACMA Past President

I have considered Rod a friend and colleague for the better part of 30 years and have both witnessed—and personally experienced—his relentless habit of expressing gratitude through handwritten notes. This man has built countless successful businesses and cultivated a wide circle of incredible friends simply because he takes the time to appreciate each person he encounters, and thoughtfully lets them know it. Rod's example and advice have also helped me build my own business through the power of handwritten thank-you notes. He truly practices what he preaches, and anyone would do well to adopt the habits presented in this book to positively impact the lives of others.

ASHLEY QUINN RCA, SPS
REALTOR® | PREMIER AGENTS NETWORK
TOP 100 TRIANGLE PRODUCERS 2024, 2025, | $150+ MILLION
INDIVIDUAL PRODUCER
AshQuinn.com

There is just something powerful about personal connection. In a digital world, we lose that, and so many things become generic rather than personal and meaningful. Rod Gray's book will demonstrate the power of a personal note or message that transcends the digital world and reaches the heart of the individual. When you use the power of the pen, it indicates to the receiver that you did what most people would not do. You went the extra mile, thought your message through, and put pen to paper. What goes out is your own heartfelt message that will make it so much more special to the person who receives it. This is a much-needed book that will change how you communicate and influence how people reciprocate. I highly recommend this new book by Rod W Gray!

CRAIG JOHNSON

Associate Pastor | Lakewood Church
Founder of Champions Clubs

The pen isn't just mightier than the sword. The pen, guided by a human hand and led with a heartfelt intent, is mightier today than ever. In an increasingly automated, AI-driven world, people are dying to hear from others. And that makes the old school practice of handwritten notes the new secret weapon in building relationships. Read Rod's book. Soak up his thoughts. Then, do what your mother told you to do and start writing handwritten notes. It will change your relationships for good.

WILLIAM VANDERBLOEMEN
Founder and CEO | Vanderbloemen Search Group

In a world where our thumbs do most of the talking, *INK* is a refreshing reminder of the heart behind handwritten words. This isn't just a book—it's a beautiful invitation to slow down and rediscover the power of putting pen to paper. From love notes to thank-you cards, Rod shows us how something as simple as ink on a page can build bridges, spark creativity, and strengthen relationships in ways that screens just can't.

Whether you're a journal junkie or someone who hasn't touched a pen in years, this book will stir something in you. It's practical, inspiring, and full of real stories that will make you smile—and maybe even grab a notebook. INK is a call to reconnect with the written word in a world that moves too fast. And I'm here for it!

MARTHA FRY
Author of *Moving Forward: Letting Go of Stuff that Will Kill You*
Marthafry.com

In his book, *INK: Discover the Power of the Pen in a Digital World,* Rod Gray captures the timeless significance of written correspondence through letters, notes, and greeting cards. Rod masterfully explores how pen and paper remain vital tools for communication and human connection, even in our increasingly digital age of cell phones and computers. This insightful book is an essential guide for anyone seeking to harness the written word's profound impact—both personally and professionally to enhance relationships in their lives.

JERRY HARDMAN
President | Landa Mobile Systems

I wholeheartedly endorse Rod Gray's compelling new book, *INK: Discover the Power of the Pen in a Digital World.*

In an era dominated by endless texts, emails, artificial intelligence, and social media noise, Rod brilliantly underscores the profound impact of handwritten correspondence. By reviving the lost art of writing letters, notes, and cards, he invites readers to slow down, step away from their screens, and reconnect with the people in their lives in a thoughtful and authentic way. This book serves as a powerful call to action, reminding us that the simple act of putting pen to paper can forge deeper connections and enrich both our lives and those of others.

Don't miss the chance to rediscover the practice of handwritten correspondence.

LINDSEY LLOYD
Vice President, Media and Production
WWE (World Wrestling Federation)

In *INK*, Rod Gray dares us to reclaim the lost art of human connection in a world hypnotized by screens. It is a timely reminder that differentiation often lies in the personal touch. Gray makes a compelling case for the handwritten note, not as a lost art, but as a competitive edge. This isn't just about nostalgia; it's about influence, trust, and the kind of connection that drives real results. Every leader, entrepreneur, and brand-builder should read this book.

WENDY K. WALTERS
Author, Ghostwriter, Editor, and Motivational Speaker
wendykwalters.com

In Memory of John Amos

TO MY DEAR FRIEND, JOHN,

To my dear friend John,

Five years may have passed, but your memory still inspires me. I cherish the handwritten note you sent before your passing, which motivated me to write this book about the enduring power of the pen in our lives. Your friendship, humor, generosity, and family have profoundly impacted me. This book honors your influence and the dignity you showed during your battle with cancer. Thank you for being an everlasting inspiration.

Ink

Acknowledgments

TO MY WIFE, AMIE, AND OUR CHILDREN—OWEN AND OLIVIA

You are my greatest sources of inspiration and motivation. I am profoundly grateful for your unwavering love and support.

TO MY MOTHER, NANCY

Thank you for always being my #1 fan. You taught me the importance of writing letters, notes, and cards to express gratitude and positively impact the lives of others. I am eternally grateful for this life lesson.

TO WENDY

This book would not have come to fruition without your invaluable contributions. I sincerely appreciate your hard work, unwavering dedication, and patience throughout the journey of bringing *INK* to life.

Ink

CONTENTS

Introduction

"In this digital world, a handwritten note is a rare and beautiful gift."

ROD GRAY

Introduction

In a world that races at lightning speed, where communication has been reduced to AI, endless texts, emails, social media posts, and videos, we find ourselves increasingly disconnected from the essence of meaningful interaction. The digital era, while undeniably powerful in its convenience, often leaves us feeling powerless against the void of genuine connection that only written correspondence can provide. *INK: Discover the Power of the Pen in a Digital World* invites you to harness the transformative power of handwritten words, empowering you to foster authentic relationships in our fast-paced digital lives.

As we delve into the chapters of this book, we will explore the rich history of handwritten communication, tracing its evolution from the earliest forms of letters to the influential figures who championed the art of writing. Each chapter reveals the powerful psychological impact of receiving a handwritten note, highlighting the emotional resonance that digital messages often fail to capture. We will discover how the pen creates personal touches that can strengthen bonds with loved ones, friends, and business associates and create lasting memories that digital interactions simply cannot replicate.

We will explore the importance of gratitude and how simple letters, notes, and cards can trigger a ripple effect, enhancing not only our relationships but also our overall well-being. Special occasions and celebrations will be emphasized, showcasing how the pen and handwritten notes can elevate these memorable moments into cherished memories. Furthermore, we will discuss the role of handwritten communication in professional settings, examining how a personal touch can empower you to stand out in an increasingly digital workplace.

Crafting the perfect handwritten note is an art form that deserves to be nurtured. We will provide practical tips on writing meaningful messages, from selecting the right pen and stationery to embracing the act of writing itself, empowering you to embrace this timeless tradition. We will also address the challenges posed by the digital age and offer guidance on inspiring the next generation to recognize the powerful beauty of letter writing.

Finally, we will delve into real-life testimonies and stories from individuals profoundly impacted by the power of handwritten words, encouraging you to take actionable steps to make handwriting a habit in your daily life. This book is not just a guide; it is a call to action. It inspires you to step away from the screens of cell phones, tablets, computers, AI, and televisions and discover the joy and empowerment that comes from putting pen to paper.

The Power of the Pen

As you journey through ***INK: Discover the Power of the Pen in a Digital World,*** remember that every handwritten correspondence possesses the power to create personal touches, forge profound connections, celebrate life's memorable moments, and express gratitude in ways that digital communication can never replicate. Let us embark on this exploration together, reigniting the art of written correspondence and embracing the invaluable relationships that can flourish through the powerful act of putting pen to paper.

"Nothing will ever replace the sincerity and individualism expressed through the handwritten word."

DAVID H. BAKER

1

CHAPTER ONE

The Evolution of Written Communication

"The pen is mightier than the sword."

EDWARD BULWER-LYTTON

Ink

1 The Evolution of Written Communication

The origins of written communication are a complex tapestry woven from the threads of human evolution, social organization, and the development of technology. The history of writing is often divided into several key periods and milestones, reflecting the gradual transition from oral to written forms of communication. Let's examine these together.

PREHISTORIC BEGINNINGS

1. Oral Tradition

   Prior to the advent of writing, humans relied on oral traditions to convey information, stories, laws, and knowledge. Oral communication is deeply rooted in human culture and likely dates back to the emergence of language itself.

2. Symbolic Expression

   Written language dates back to when humans began to use symbols, as evidenced by cave paintings found in places like Lascaux, France, and Altamira, Spain. These artworks served as a form of nonverbal communication, conveying ideas and stories through imagery. Similarly, engraved objects, such as the Ishango bone from the Congo, suggest early attempts at recording information.

THE DAWN OF WRITING SYSTEMS

1. Proto-Writing (circa 4000-3000 BCE)

   The transition from purely oral communication to written forms began with proto-writing systems, where symbols were used to convey meaning but did not represent spoken language phonetically. Examples include the Jiahu symbols in China, which date back to around 6600 BCE, and the Vinča symbols in Southeastern Europe.

2. Cuneiform (circa 3200 BCE)

   The Sumerians of Mesopotamia are credited with developing one of the earliest known writing systems, cuneiform. This system involved making wedge-shaped impressions on clay tablets using a stylus. Initially used for record-keeping, such as tracking grain and trade, cuneiform evolved to encompass literature, legal codes, and historical records.

3. Hieroglyphs (circa 3100 BCE)

   In ancient Egypt, hieroglyphs emerged as a formal writing system that combined logographic and alphabetic elements. Hieroglyphs were used for religious texts, monumental inscriptions, and administrative records. The Rosetta Stone, discovered in 1799, played a crucial role in deciphering these symbols.

4. Chinese Characters (circa 1200 BCE)

The earliest known Chinese writing dates back to the Shang dynasty, with oracle bone inscriptions used for divination. Over time, this evolved into a complex system of characters that represented words or morphemes, forming the basis of modern Chinese script.

THE ALPHABETIC REVOLUTION

1. Phoenician Alphabet (circa 1050 BCE)

The Phoenicians developed one of the first alphabetic writing systems, which used a limited number of characters to represent sounds. This innovation greatly simplified writing and made literacy more accessible. The Phoenician alphabet influenced many subsequent writing systems, including Greek and Latin.

2. Greek and Latin Alphabets (circa 800 BCE)

The Greeks adopted and adapted the Phoenician alphabet around the 8th century BCE, adding vowels to create a more phonetic system. The Latin alphabet emerged from the Greek script and became the foundation for many modern alphabets used in Western languages.

WRITING IN DIVERSE CULTURES

1. Mesoamerican Scripts (circa 1200 – 400 BCE)

   In the Americas, the Olmec civilization and later cultures like the Maya developed their own writing systems, including the Maya glyphs, which were used for recording history, rituals, and astronomy.

2. Indus Valley Script (circa 1600-1900 BCE)

   The Indus Valley civilization in present-day Pakistan and northwest India developed a script that remains undeciphered. While numerous seals and inscriptions have been found, the lack of understanding of the language hampers insights into their written communication.

THE ROLE OF WRITING IN CIVILIZATION

1. Record Keeping and Administration

   The development of writing facilitated the growth of complex societies. Written records allowed for more sophisticated trade, legal systems, and governance. Kings and rulers used writing to issue decrees, maintain records of taxes, and document laws.

2. Literature and Education

As writing became more widespread, it gave rise to literature, philosophy, and science. ***The Epic of Gilgamesh,*** the ***Iliad***, and the works of Confucius represent some of the earliest written literature. Schools began to emerge, teaching literacy and the arts of writing.

THE EVOLUTION OF WRITING TOOLS AND MATERIALS

1. Writing Materials

Initially, writing was inscribed on clay tablets, stone, or bone. Over time, materials evolved to include papyrus in Egypt, parchment in the Mediterranean, and eventually paper, invented in China during the Han dynasty (circa 100 CE). The development of ink and writing instruments, such as quills and brushes, further advanced the practice of writing.

2. Printing Revolution

The invention of the printing press by Johannes Gutenberg in the 15th century marked a turning point in written communication. It allowed for the mass production of books, making literature and knowledge more accessible to the general public and facilitating the spread of ideas during the Renaissance and beyond.

INFLUENTIAL HISTORICAL FIGURES WHO VALUED HANDWRITTEN CORRESPONDENCE

Throughout history, numerous notable individuals have recognized the unique power of handwritten communication to convey thoughts and emotions in ways that printed text often cannot. Here are several influential figures renowned for their handwritten personal notes, letters, and cards:

1. George H.W. Bush

   The 41st President of the United States was well known for his practice of writing personal notes to friends, colleagues, and political adversaries, reflecting his belief in the power of personal communication to foster relationships.

2. Abraham Lincoln

   The 16th President of the United States often penned personal letters, including heartfelt notes of condolence and encouragement, revealing his compassion and deep commitment to the nation during times of crisis.

3. Martin Luther King, Jr

   The Civil rights icon wrote many letters, more notably the "Letter from the Birmingham Jail." This letter articulated his views on civil rights, justice, and nonviolent protests. His writings have inspired generations to work for equality and justice.

4. Mother Teresa

Known for her compassion and humanitarian work, she wrote letters of encouragement and support to those in need, as well as to her friends and colleagues, inspiring them to continue their work in service of the poor.

5. Ronald Reagan

The 40th President of the United States may have been the most prolific correspondent of any American president since Thomas Jefferson. The total number of letters written over his lifetime exceeds approximately 10,000. Collectively, President Reagan's letters revealed his character and thinking like no other source and added a personal touch to his presidency.

6. Helen Keller

Despite her disabilities, Keller wrote numerous letters advocating for the rights of people with disabilities, women's suffrage, and social justice. Her heartfelt letters inspired countless individuals and brought attention to important social issues.

7. Vincent van Gogh

The Dutch painter is famous for his letters to his friends and family, which detailed his artistic processes, personal struggles, and reflections on his life and work.

8. Frida Kahlo

The Mexican artist expressed her emotions and thoughts through letters, often addressing friends and fellow artists, reflecting her passionate and complex personality.

9. Mark Twain

The American author and humorist was known for his witty and engaging letters, which he wrote to friends, family, and fellow writers, sharing anecdotes and social commentary.

10. Princess Diana

The late British royal was known for her personal touch in correspondence, often writing heartfelt letters to individuals and organizations, showcasing her compassion and commitment to charitable causes.

These historical figures are but a few who used handwritten letters and notes not only as communication tools but also as a means to build and sustain personal connections, allowing a glimpse into their thoughts, feelings, and values.

They also understood that the nuances of handwriting often convey sentiments that digital communication cannot replicate. The imperfections of penmanship, the choice of paper, and the tactile act of writing contribute to a personal touch that reflects care and attentiveness. Their appreciation for handwritten communication serves as a reminder of the value of taking the time to express ourselves in this timeless manner.

Real Life Story

TWO HISTORIC AMERICAN FIGURES CONNECT THROUGH A HANDWRITTEN LETTER

The famous story of legendary American singer and actor Elvis Presley and the 27th President of the United States, Richard Nixon, revolves around a meeting that took place on December 21, 1970, at the White House in Washington, DC. Elvis, who was a huge fan of President Nixon, wrote a handwritten letter to him and showed up at the White House entrance unannounced, requesting a meeting with the president. In the letter, Elvis expressed his desire to help combat drug abuse in America and offered his support for Nixon's efforts.

Elvis' cursive letter was written on six pieces of American Airlines stationery from his home and highlighted his concerns about the youth of America and the influence of drugs. Nixon's staff arranged the meeting, and it became a memorable moment in pop culture history.

During the meeting, Elvis presented Nixon with a gift: a Colt .45 pistol, which he had brought along as a token of appreciation. The meeting was brief, lasting about 30 minutes, but it was significant as it brought together two iconic figures from American culture in a rather unexpected way.

The handwritten note itself has become a notable piece of memorabilia, reflecting the intersection of music, politics, and celebrity culture during that era. The entire event is often remembered for its surreal nature and the unlikely relationship between the King of Rock 'n' Roll and the President of the United States.

Following is the transcript of this famous handwritten letter by Elvis:

Dear Mr. President,

First, I would like to introduce myself. I am Elvis Presley, and admire you and have great respect for your office. I talked to Vice President Agnew in Palm Springs three weeks ago and expressed my concern for our country. The drug culture, the hippie elements, the SDS, Black Panthers, etc., do not consider me their enemy or, as they call it, "the establishment." I call it America, and I love it.

Sir, I can and will be of any service that I can to help the country. I have no concerns or motives other than helping the country out.

So, I wish not to be given a title or an appointed position. I can and will do more good if I were made a Federal Agent at Large, and I will help out by doing it my way through my communications with people of all ages. First and foremost, I am an entertainer, but all I need is the Federal credentials. I am currently on a plane with Senator

George Murphy, and we have been discussing the problems our country is faced with.

Sir, I am staying at the Washington Hotel, Room 505-506-507. I have two men who work with me by the name of Jerry Schilling and Sonny West. I am registered under the name of Jon Burrows. I will be here for as long as it takes to obtain the credentials of a Federal Agent. I have done an in-depth study of drug abuse and Communist brainwashing techniques, and I am right in the middle of the whole thing where I can and will do the most good.

I am glad to help just so long as it is kept very private. You can have your staff or whomever call me anytime today, tonight, or tomorrow. I was nominated this coming year one of America's Ten Most Outstanding Young Men. That will take place on January 18 in my home town of Memphis, Tennessee. I am sending you the short autobiography about myself so you can better understand this approach. I would love to meet you just to say hello, if you're not too busy.

Respectfully,

Elvis Presley

P.S. I believe that you, Sir, were one of the Top Ten Outstanding Men of America also.

I have a personal gift for you that I would like to present to you and you can accept it or I will keep it for you until you can take it.

Mr. President,

These are my PVT numbers:

Beverly Hills	*278-3496*
	278-9535
Palm Springs	*325-3241*
Pvt #	
Memphis	*397-4427*
Pvt. #	*398-4882*
	398-9722
Col P.S. #	*325-4781*
Col B.H. #	*274-8498*
Col. Off M.E.M.	*870-0370*

WASHINGTON HOTEL PHONE ME 85900

Room 505-506

Under the name of Jon Burrows

PRIVATE

AND CONFIDENTIAL

Attn. President Nixon

via Sen. George Murphy

from

Elvis Presley[1]

1 Elvis' Letter to Nixon (Transcript) from the National Archives. Retrieved on 01.06.2025 at https://www.archives.gov/historical-docs/elvis-letter-to-nixon.

The Power of the Pen

The evolution of written correspondence reflects humanity's enduring quest for connection and understanding. From ancient tokens to digital messages, each phase of this journey highlights our adaptability and creativity in overcoming the challenges of communication. As we move forward, the future of written correspondence will undoubtedly continue to evolve, shaped by new technologies and cultural shifts, yet remaining rooted in our fundamental need to communicate. Never forget the power handwritten words have in our lives and in history.

"No emailed message or attached Word document—no matter how heartfelt or well-composed—compares with a letter ... validated by an official postmark that adds the important context of date and place ... Finding and reading handwritten letters from nearly 100 years ago is perhaps the closest thing we have to a time machine."

EDITORIAL, VALLEY NEWS

REFLECTION QUESTIONS

These reflection questions are designed to help you internalize the concepts presented in this chapter and consider practical ways to apply the art of handwritten communication in your own life.

1. Personal Connection

    Reflect on a handwritten letter or note you have received that made a significant impact on you. What emotions did it evoke, and why do you think it resonated with you so deeply?

2. Historical Influence

    Consider one of the historical figures mentioned in this chapter. How did their use of handwritten communication shape their relationships or influence their legacy? What can you learn from their approach to communication?

3. Current Practices

    In your daily life, how often do you engage in handwritten correspondence? What barriers do you face in adopting this practice more regularly?

4. Emotional Expression

Think about a recent interaction where you communicated via text or email. How might a handwritten note have changed the tone or depth of that communication?

5. Reviving the Art

What steps can you take to incorporate handwritten communication into your routine? Consider setting a goal for yourself, such as sending one handwritten note per week.

6. Value of Time

Reflect on the time and effort involved in writing by hand compared to typing. How does this time investment contribute to the perceived value of the message?

7. Impact on Relationships

How do you believe radical empathy can be enhanced through handwritten correspondence? What specific ways can you apply this principle to strengthen your personal and professional relationships?

8. Cultural Shifts

How has the rise of digital communication affected your perception of the value of handwritten notes? Do you think there is a cultural shift occurring that may lead to a resurgence in handwritten correspondence?

9. Creative Exploration

If you were to write a letter to your future self, what thoughts, hopes, or reflections would you include? How does the act of writing by hand change the way you express those thoughts?

10. Legacy of Handwriting

What legacy do you hope to leave in your own handwritten communications? How might your handwriting reflect your personality and values in a way that digital communication cannot?

2

CHAPTER TWO

The Psychological Impact of Handwritten Notes

"A handwritten note is a gift from the heart."

SARAH FAULKNER

2

The Psychological Impact of Handwritten Notes

In a fast-paced world dominated by instant messaging and digital communication, the act of receiving a handwritten note, greeting card, or letter has become a rare and delightful experience. While emails and texts are quick and efficient, they often lack the warmth and personal touch that a handwritten note provides. Studies have shown that when someone receives a handwritten note, it triggers a unique emotional response that can enhance feelings of gratitude, connection, and overall well-being. This chapter explores the psychological benefits of handwritten notes, delving into why they resonate so deeply with recipients.

THE UNIQUE EMOTIONAL RESPONSE

When a person receives a handwritten note, they are not merely reading words on a page; they are experiencing a tangible expression of thoughtfulness and effort. The very act of handwriting requires time and intention, elements that are often absent in the immediacy of digital communication. This investment of time translates into a deeper emotional connection. Research reveals that receiving a handwritten note can evoke feelings of joy and surprise, igniting a sense of appreciation that is often more profound than that elicited by digital messages.

The psychology behind this response is rooted in the concept of effort justification. When someone takes the time to write a note by hand, the recipient perceives that effort as a sign of care and importance. This perception fosters a sense of value in the relationship, reinforcing social bonds and enhancing feelings of belonging. In a world where interactions can often feel superficial, the authenticity of a handwritten note stands out, creating an emotional response that is hard to replicate.

Receiving a handwritten letter, note, or greeting card evokes a deeply emotional and unique response that resonates on multiple levels, intertwining nostalgia, intimacy, and a sense of connection.

A DETAILED EXPLORATION OF THESE EMOTIONS:

1. Nostalgia and Sentimentality

The tactile nature of a handwritten letter often prompts feelings of nostalgia. In an age dominated by digital communication, the sight of penmanship can evoke images of simpler times when people relied on the written word to express their feelings. The unique curves and flourishes of the writer's handwriting carry personal history; they may remind the recipient of past relationships or shared experiences. This nostalgia can transport the reader to a moment when they, too, wrote or received similar letters, rekindling emotions tied to those memories. Even if this is a new experience for them, receiving a handwritten note can shape a person's perception and stir positive sentiment. It is memorable.

2. Personal Connection

A handwritten letter is inherently personal. The effort and time it takes to write by hand—choosing the right paper, selecting a pen, and crafting each sentence—communicate a level of care that digital messages often lack. This investment creates a deep sense of value; the recipient feels that the sender has prioritized them enough to take this time. The physicality of the letter—the texture of the paper, the ink's flow—adds a layer of intimacy that conveys affection and thoughtfulness.

3. Surprise and Delight

In a world where communication is often rapid and impersonal, receiving an unexpected handwritten note can generate a delightful surprise. The anticipation of opening an envelope, the crinkle of paper or the opening of a card, and the unveiling of the message can trigger feelings of excitement and curiosity. This joy is heightened by the rarity of such gestures in contemporary society, making the experience feel special and memorable.

4. Emotional Resonance

Research published in the journal ***Psychological Science*** indicates that receiving personalized communication, such as handwritten letters, can evoke feelings of happiness and increase overall well-being. This emotional uplift can lead to reduced stress and anxiety levels. Handwritten letters often convey emotions in a way that typed messages cannot. The nuances of the writer's feelings—joy, love, sorrow, or encouragement—are often more palpable. The imperfections of handwriting can reflect vulnerability, making the message feel more genuine and heartfelt. The recipient may find themselves immersed in the emotions conveyed within the text, fostering a deeper understanding of the sender's thoughts and feelings. This emotional resonance can also evoke empathy, allowing the reader to connect with the sender's experiences and emotions.

5. Validation and Affirmation

Receiving a handwritten note can serve as a form of validation. It signifies that someone has taken the time to acknowledge the recipient's existence, and it honors their thoughts and feelings. This effort can reinforce self-worth and provide emotional support, reminding the recipient that they are valued and remembered. Especially during difficult times, such a letter can serve as a lifeline, offering comfort and reassurance.

6. Symbol of Commitment

In relationships, whether romantic, familial, or platonic, a handwritten letter can symbolize commitment and dedication. It shows a willingness to invest in the relationship and communicate thoughtfully. This commitment can strengthen bonds, as the recipient understands that the sender values their connection enough to express their feelings in a lasting form.

Real-Life Story

THE EMOTIONAL IMPACT OF CARDS AND LETTERS

In 2017, my family experienced a life-altering event when our home in Cypress, Texas, was completely flooded due to the record-breaking rains from Hurricane Harvey. The devastation was overwhelming; we did not have flood insurance and faced more than $90,000 in damages and expenses. The emotional toll was just as significant as the financial burden, as we found ourselves displaced and living in a hotel, grappling with the uncertainty of our future.

During this challenging time, something remarkable happened. We began receiving an outpouring of handwritten notes and cards from family, friends, co-workers, customers, former clients, and even strangers. Each envelope that arrived in the mail became a beacon of hope amidst the chaos of our lives.

As I opened each note, I took the time to read every single word. These were not just pieces of paper; they were heartfelt messages infused with compassion and empathy. Some contained prayers, while others offered words of encouragement. Many included financial support to help us navigate the difficult months ahead. Each note was a reminder that we were not alone in our struggle, reinforcing that there were people who cared deeply about our well-being and wanted to help us through this trying time.

The impact of these handwritten notes was profound. They served as a catalyst for healing, reminding us of the kindness and generosity that exists in the world, even in the face of adversity. Each note we received lifted our spirits and provided comfort, helping us to cope with the stress and uncertainty of rebuilding our lives. The simple act of someone taking the time to write to us and share their thoughts and support created a sense of connection that was invaluable.

Now, several years later, I still have every one of those notes carefully stored in a box inside my nightstand by my bedside. Periodically, I pull them out and read through them once again. Each message transports me back to that tumultuous time, but rather than feeling the pain of loss, I am reminded of the love and support that surrounded us. The words echo in my mind—affirmations of hope, resilience, and community.

The psychological impact of receiving those handwritten notes cannot be overstated. They provided not only emotional support but also a sense of belonging and reassurance. But don't just take my word for it. According to the American Psychological Association, social interactions that promote feelings of connection and support help lower stress levels. Receiving a handwritten letter can elicit positive emotions and reinforce supportive relationships, contributing to lower stress and better mental health.

In a world that often feels disconnected, these notes were tangible reminders that human connection and kindness can shine through even the darkest moments.

As I reflect on this experience, I realize that handwritten notes are more than just words on paper—they have the power to heal, uplift, and inspire. In times of difficulty, they can become a lifeline, reminding us of the love that surrounds us and the strength we possess to rebuild our lives. The art of handwritten communication is a gift that can create lasting positive effects, not just for the recipient but for everyone involved.

Handwritten notes are more than just words on paper—they have the power to heal, uplift, and inspire.

INCREASED FEELINGS OF GRATITUDE

One of the most significant psychological benefits of receiving a handwritten note is the increase in feelings of gratitude. Gratitude is a powerful emotion that contributes to overall mental health and well-being. Studies have shown that expressing and receiving gratitude can lead to higher levels of happiness, reduced stress, and improved relationships.

When someone receives a handwritten note, they not only feel recognized, but they also feel appreciated. This acknowledgment can shift their perspective, prompting them to reflect on the positive aspects of their lives and the people who contribute to their happiness. Gratitude creates a cycle of positivity; when we feel grateful, we are more likely to express gratitude in return, strengthening the bonds we share with others.

The act of writing thank-you notes, for example, has been shown to enhance feelings of gratitude not only for the recipient but also for the sender. This reciprocal exchange fosters a culture of appreciation and connection, demonstrating how handwritten notes can have a ripple effect on emotional well-being.

STRENGTHENING CONNECTIONS

Handwritten notes also play a vital role in fostering meaningful connections between individuals. A study from the University of California, Los Angeles (UCLA) found that social support is crucial for mental health. Handwritten letters can enhance feelings of social connection and belonging, which are essential for emotional health. The tangible nature of a handwritten note can create a stronger bond than digital communication, which is more prone to misinterpretations and misunderstandings. The clarity and sincerity of handwritten messages can bridge gaps and strengthen relationships.

When someone receives a handwritten note, it often serves as a reminder of the sender's presence in their life. This reminder can be particularly meaningful during challenging times, as it provides a sense of support and encouragement. Notes can serve as tangible tokens of affection in ways that a saved email or text just cannot come close to. Physical notes remind recipients that they are valued and cared for long after they are received.

Moreover, the act of writing a note can also benefit the sender. The process of writing by hand encourages the one composing the note to reflect on the recipient and the nature of their relationship, fostering a deeper understanding of the connection they share. This mindfulness not only enhances the quality of the note but also enriches the sender's emotional experience, creating a bond that is felt on both sides.

Real-Life Story

HANDWRITTEN LETTERS WRITTEN BY WORLD LEADERS STRENGTHENED RELATIONSHIPS BETWEEN COUNTRIES

There are several instances in history where handwritten letters between leaders of countries have played a significant role in strengthening relationships between countries or resolving conflicts. The following are a few notable examples:

1. Franklin D. Roosevelt and Winston Churchill

During World War II, U.S. Franklin D. Roosevelt (32nd President of the United States) and British Prime Minister Winston Churchill exchanged numerous letters. Their correspondence helped to solidify the alliance between the United States and the United Kingdom, facilitating cooperation in military strategy and post-war planning. Their letters demonstrated mutual respect and a shared vision for the future, which was crucial in uniting their countries against the Axis powers.

2. Ronald Reagan and Mikhail Gorbachev

In the 1980s, Ronald Reagan (40th President of the United States) and Soviet General Secretary Mikhail Gorbachev engaged in a series of letters that contributed to the de-escalation of Cold War tensions. Their written communications helped to build trust and understanding, leading to significant arms control agreements, such as the Intermediate-Range Nuclear Forces Treaty in 1987.

3. John F. Kennedy and Nikita Khrushchev

During the Cuban Missile Crisis in 1962, John F. Kennedy (35th President of the United States) and Soviet Premier Nikita Khrushchev exchanged letters that were critical in navigating the crisis. The correspondence allowed them to communicate directly and rapidly, which helped to prevent a potential nuclear confrontation. Their willingness to engage in dialogue through letters was instrumental in reaching a resolution.

4. Queen Elizabeth II and Dwight D. Eisenhower

The correspondence between Queen Elizabeth II and Dwight D. Eisenhower (34th President of the United States) during the 1950s helped to strengthen the "Special Relationship" between the United Kingdom and the United States. Their letters reflected a personal rapport that transcended political differences and reinforced the alliance between their nations.

5. The "Letters of Reconciliation" between North and South Korea

In more recent times, leaders from North and South Korea, including Kim Jong-un and Moon Jae-in, have exchanged letters that reflected efforts to improve relations and reduce tensions on the Korean Peninsula. These communications have played a role in diplomatic initiatives and summits aimed at achieving peace and reconciliation.

These examples illustrate that handwritten letters can serve as powerful tools for diplomacy, enabling leaders to express intentions, build trust, and navigate complex international relationships. Whether as above between leaders of nations or with family members, friends, colleagues, or clients, handwritten letters clarify ideas and positions and bring people closer together in positive ways.

THE NEUROSCIENCE OF HANDWRITTEN CORRESPONDENCE

The neuroscience of writing and receiving handwritten correspondence involves several cognitive, emotional, and neurological processes. Here are some key aspects to consider:

1. Motor Skills and Brain Activity

Writing by hand involves complex fine motor skills that engage various parts of the brain, particularly the motor cortex. The physical act of writing activates neural pathways related to hand-eye coordination and fine motor control.

Neurological Activation Studies using functional MRI (fMRI) have shown that handwriting activates areas of the brain associated with language processing and memory, unlike typing, which may engage different neural circuits.

2. Cognitive Processing

Handwriting has been linked to better retention and understanding of information. The process of writing by hand requires more cognitive engagement, which can enhance learning, memory encoding, and retrieval.

Handwriting allows for a more personal and creative expression. The unique characteristics of one's handwriting can reflect individual personality traits and emotional states.

3. Emotional Connection

Handwritten letters carry a personal touch as they often carry a sense of intimacy and thoughtfulness that digital correspondence may lack.

4. Social and Psychological Aspects

We have demonstrated that handwritten correspondence can strengthen social bonds. It fosters a sense of connection and can be more impactful than digital communication, as it demonstrates time and effort.

5. Therapeutic Benefits

Writing letters by hand is sometimes used in therapeutic settings. It can serve as a tool for self-reflection and emotional processing, helping individuals articulate and sort their thoughts and feelings.

6. Cognitive Load

The slower pace of handwriting compared to typing can lead to deeper processing of information. This slower method allows individuals to think critically about what they are writing.

The Power of the Pen

Handwritten notes hold a unique psychological power that can enhance our emotional lives in profound ways. They evoke feelings of joy, gratitude, and connection, reminding us of the importance of personal touch in our relationships. Taking the time to write and send a handwritten note can be a powerful, transformative act for both the recipient and the sender.

REFLECTION QUESTIONS

As we navigate our busy lives, let us cherish the emotional impact of handwritten communication and embrace the opportunity to foster deeper connections through the simple act of writing. These reflection questions are designed to help you internalize the lessons from this chapter and consider practical ways to apply the power of handwritten communication in your own life and relationships.

1. Reflection

Reflect on a time when you received a handwritten note or card that made a significant difference in your life. What emotions did it evoke, and how did it impact your perspective during that time?

2. Expressing Support

How can you incorporate the practice of sending handwritten notes into your own life, especially during times of crisis or hardship for others? What specific messages of support or encouragement would you want to convey?

3. Emotional Connection

Consider the difference between receiving a handwritten note versus a digital message. How does the physicality of a handwritten note enhance the emotional connection and support it provides?

4. Building Community

In what ways can you use handwritten communication to strengthen your relationships with family, friends, or colleagues? What steps can you take to create a culture of kindness and support within your community?

5. Legacy of Kindness

How do you want to be remembered when it comes to your interactions with others? What role can handwritten letters, notes, and greeting cards play in building your legacy of kindness and support?

6. Healing Power

Is someone close to you facing a challenging situation? How could handwritten correspondence from you serve as a source of comfort and encouragement during this time?

7. Gratitude Practice

Reflect on the impact of gratitude in your life. Consider crafting handwritten thank-you notes to those who have supported you. How could this enhance your feelings of gratitude and foster deeper connections with those for whom you are grateful?

8. Mindfulness in Writing

When handwriting a note, you are more likely to be present and intentional in your choice of words. What mindfulness techniques might help you focus on the recipient's feelings and needs?

9. Encouraging Others

You can encourage others in your life to embrace the practice of handwritten communication. Would you consider starting a handwritten note exchange among friends or family?

10. Long-term Impact

Do you keep handwritten letters and cards? Do you have a special place to collect them? This practice allows you to periodically revisit and reflect on the messages you've received over the years. What emotions or insights do you think this practice would evoke?

Handwritten letters
offer a personal touch
that digital messages
often lack, making the
recipient feel truly valued.

3

CHAPTER THREE

Building Relationships Through Handwritten Correspondence

"In a world of digital communication, a handwritten note is a heartfelt reminder someone took the time to care."

BELINDA THOMAS

Ink

3

Building Relationships Through Handwritten Correspondence

In today's fast-paced, technology-driven world, communication often feels rushed and transactional. Text messages, emails, and social media interactions can lack the warmth and intimacy that foster genuine connections. Tone can be difficult to convey digitally, so the meaning of the message can get lost in translation. In contrast, using pen and ink allows individuals to express their thoughts, feelings, and appreciation clearly in a meaningful way. Handwritten notes offer a personal touch that can significantly deepen personal and professional relationships for several reasons:

1. It Conveys Warmth

Handwritten communication feels more personal and intimate than digital messages. It shows that the sender took the time and effort to express themselves thoughtfully, which can make the recipient feel valued and appreciated. The effort involved in writing by hand can convey sincerity and warmth, fostering deeper connections. The act of opening an envelope and the feel of the card or paper lights up different parts of the brain than opening an email. There is a stronger and more lasting emotional connection made.

2. It Aids in Conflict Resolution

Handwritten communication can serve as a tool for conflict resolution. A study in the ***Journal of Social and Personal Relationships*** suggested that expressing feelings through letters can help individuals articulate their thoughts and emotions better, leading to improved understanding and resolution of conflicts within relationships.

3. It Makes You Stand Out

We receive a barrage of digital communication every day. Among a myriad of electronic emails and texts—many that cause stress or even irritate—receiving a handwritten note stands out and leaves a lasting and positive impression. Handwritten letters are more likely to be sorted and categorized by the brain and make it to long-term memory as opposed to digital ones.

4. It Encourages Reciprocity

Sending a handwritten note can encourage recipients to respond in kind, fostering a cycle of thoughtful communication that strengthens the relationship. If your note is asking for a favor or containing a request, going the extra mile of using pen and ink to ask is more likely to get you a favorable reply.

5. It Fosters Community and Belonging

Research published in the ***Journal of Community Psychology*** emphasizes the importance of community support for mental well-being. Handwritten notes can foster a sense of belonging and community, which is vital for professional and personal relationships and family cohesion.

6. It Celebrates Milestones

Sending paper greeting cards for birthdays, anniversaries, or other significant events demonstrates that you care about the person's life and achievements, which helps to strengthen bonds. People keep cards and letters. Emails get buried under the mountain of junk, spam, newsletters, bills, and inquiries.

7. It Provides Professional Distinction

One way to unleash the power of pen and ink is in a professional context. In business, handwritten notes set you apart from others. They demonstrate professionalism, thoughtfulness, and attention to detail, which can enhance your reputation and strengthen client or colleague relationships. They get you noticed and remembered.

8. It Builds Trust

As AI and Chat GPT flood everyday communication, knowing that you sat down and used your brain to compose your thoughts has an authenticity about it that cannot be discounted. Therefore, handwritten communication can help build trust. It signals that you are willing to invest time and effort—your own effort—into your communication. This enhances the relationship.

9. It Encourages Reflection

The act of writing by hand can be reflective, allowing the sender to think more deeply about their words. This increased self-awareness can lead to more meaningful communication that resonates with the recipient.

10. It Creates Traditions

Establishing a habit of sending handwritten notes or cards can create a tradition within personal or professional relationships, reinforcing connections over time. It is something you can become known for—remembered for.

Handwritten letters, notes, and greeting cards are your secret weapon once you learn how to unleash their power. They serve as powerful tools for expressing feelings, recognizing milestones, and building trust. They foster stronger, more meaningful connections in both personal and professional settings.

> Handwritten correspondence is your secret weapon to foster stronger, more meaningful connections.

I want to share some poignant stories of individuals who have strengthened their bonds with family and friends through the simple yet powerful act of writing.

Real Life Stories

THE POWER OF A SIMPLE THANK YOU

Consider the story of Maria, a nurse who had just moved to Mission, Texas. Feeling isolated in her new environment, she sought to connect with her neighbors. Inspired by her grandmother, who had always written thank-you notes for small gestures, Maria decided to pen a heartfelt note to each of her neighbors after they welcomed her with baked goods and warm smiles.

In her notes, Maria expressed her gratitude for their kindness and shared a little about herself. To her surprise, the handwritten notes sparked a wave of responses. Neighbors reciprocated with notes of their own, sharing their stories and inviting her to join them for coffee or neighborhood events. What began as a simple thank-you transformed into a network of friendships that enriched her life. Maria learned that the authenticity and effort behind a handwritten note could bridge the gap between strangers, forging connections that might have otherwise remained superficial.

REKINDLING OLD FRIENDSHIPS

Let's look at David from Tampa, Florida who had lost touch with his college roommate, Sam, after graduation from Florida State University. Life had taken them in different directions, and their friendship had dwindled. One day, feeling nostalgic, David decided to reach out to Sam the old-fashioned way—

by writing him a letter, putting a stamp on the envelope, and mailing it at the post office.

In his letter, David reminisced about their shared experiences, the late-night study sessions, and the adventures they had together. He expressed how much he valued their friendship and missed the connection they once had. To David's delight, Sam responded with an equally heartfelt letter filled with memories and updates about his life. This exchange reignited their friendship, leading to regular digital correspondence through texts and e-mails and, eventually, in-person reunions. David discovered that the tactile nature of a handwritten letter carried a weight that digital communication simply could not match, reinvigorating a bond that had been dormant for years.

NURTURING FAMILY CONNECTIONS

Hailing from Chicago, Illinois, Colette is a mother of three who wanted to cultivate a stronger connection with her children. In a world where distractions abound, she felt that meaningful conversations often got lost in the shuffle of daily life. Inspired to change this, Colette initiated a family tradition of writing notes to each other.

Every week, each family member would write a note to another member of the family, sharing thoughts, encouragement, or simply expressing love. Colette's children, initially hesitant, soon embraced the practice. The notes became a cherished way for them to communicate their feelings, discuss their challenges, and celebrate each other's achievements. Over time, this tradition not only fostered open communication but also created a safe space for vulnerability and emotional expression, strengthening their family ties.

CELEBRATING LIFE TOGETHER ACROSS THE MILES

Handwritten cards and notes are a powerful way to commemorate life together across the miles, as illustrated by the touching relationship between my daughter, Olivia, from College Station, Texas, and her Nana, Nancy, who resides in Raleigh, North Carolina. Each year, Olivia eagerly anticipates the arrival of her Nana's birthday card, meticulously crafted in beautiful cursive and filled with heartfelt, encouraging words. This birthday tradition has become a profound source of inspiration for Olivia. As the years pass, these cards grow increasingly precious, especially as Olivia recognizes that her Nana will not always be by her side. She finds comfort in the collection of cards and letters she has amassed over time; they serve as tangible reminders of their bond and the values her grandmother has imparted.

In a tribute to her Nana, Olivia has tattooed her Nana's handwritten words on her ankle, which read, "Love you lots!" These cherished words will remain with Olivia long after her Nana has gone, ensuring that their connection endures through time. (And I'll wager that Olivia will continue this tradition and send handwritten cards to her children and grandchildren as her future unfolds.)

LEAVING A LEGACY

After his passing in 2015, former University of North Carolina at Chapel Hill Tar Heels head legendary basketball coach Dean Smith left a handwritten note to each former player that said, "Enjoy a dinner out, compliments of Coach Dean Smith." With the note, he also left a monetary gift of $200 in his estate for each of his 180 former players and managers. This was a sincere expression of Coach Smith's appreciation for his former players' contributions to the team, UNC, and their time together. This gesture reflected Smith's deep commitment to his players and his legacy as a coach at the University of North Carolina. Many players framed this final note from Coach Smith and, along with the memories they shared together, will cherish it for years to come.

THE RIPPLE EFFECT

Handwritten notes can be used therapeutically to improve relationship dynamics. Research indicates that expressive writing can help individuals process emotions, leading to healthier communication patterns within families and friendships. The stories of Maria, David, Colette, Olivia, and Coach Smith illustrate the profound impact that handwritten notes can have on building and nurturing relationships. These simple acts of writing can create ripples of connection that extend far beyond the initial exchange. When one person takes the time to express their thoughts and feelings through a handwritten note, it encourages the recipient to do the same, fostering a culture of appreciation and open communication.

We could use a little more civility and grace in our society, wouldn't you agree?

The stories shared in this chapter highlight how a few words written with intention can transform connections, rekindle friendships, and nurture family bonds. In a world that often prioritizes speed and efficiency over authenticity, handwritten notes remind us of the value of personal touch. They invite us to slow down, reflect, and genuinely connect with those we care about.

The Power of the Pen

As we navigate our busy lives, let us not underestimate the power of a handwritten note to strengthen our relationships. In an age where communication is often fleeting, handwritten notes offer a timeless way to express our feelings and build lasting connections. By embracing this practice, we can deepen our relationships, enrich our lives, and create a sense of community that transcends the barriers of modern communication. So, pick up a pen, write a note, and watch as the simple act of writing fosters deeper connections in your life.

REFLECTION QUESTIONS

These reflection questions are designed to help you internalize the concepts from this chapter and consider practical ways to apply the power of handwritten notes to enhance your relationships and communication.

1. Personal Experience

   Reflect on a handwritten note you have received that made a significant impact on your relationship with the sender. What did it mean to you, and how did it deepen your connection?

2. Expressing Gratitude

   Think about someone in your life who has made a difference to you recently. How might a handwritten thank-you note enhance your appreciation for their support or kindness?

3. Rekindling Connections

   Are there any old friends or acquaintances you've lost touch with? How could you use a handwritten letter to reconnect and revive those relationships? What memories or experiences would you want to share?

4. Family Communication

Consider how you currently communicate with your family. How might introducing handwritten notes into your family dynamics improve your relationships and encourage open dialogue?

5. Celebrating Milestones

Reflect on significant events in your life or the lives of loved ones. How can you use handwritten notes to commemorate these moments in a meaningful way? What traditions could you start or continue?

6. The Ripple Effect

How do you believe sending a handwritten note might inspire others to communicate more authentically? What small actions can you take to create a culture of appreciation within your social or professional circles?

7. Intentional Communication

When writing a handwritten note, how can you ensure that your message is thoughtful and sincere? What strategies can you employ to engage more deeply with the recipient's feelings and experiences?

8. Overcoming Hesitation

If you feel hesitant about writing handwritten notes, what fears or barriers are holding you back? How can you address these concerns and embrace the practice of heartfelt communication?

9. Creating a Writing Habit

What steps can you take to incorporate handwritten communication into your regular routine? Consider setting a goal for how many notes you would like to write each month.

10. Long-term Impact

As you think about your relationships, how might the practice of writing handwritten notes create lasting memories and foster deeper connections over time? What legacy do you hope to build through your written correspondence?

Sending a greeting card can brighten someone's day and create a lasting memory.

CHAPTER FOUR

4

The Power of Gratitude

"Gratitude is not only the greatest of virtues, but the parent of all others."

CICERO

4
The Power of Gratitude

Our culture is overshadowed by negativity and stress. Cultivating a mindset of gratitude serves as a powerful antidote, and writing thank-you notes is a great way to develop gratitude. This chapter explores the transformative nature of gratitude, emphasizing its importance in recognizing both the big and small blessings in our lives. By acknowledging the kindness of others and the gifts and efforts we often take for granted, we can create a ripple effect that enhances our well-being and enriches our relationships.

GRATITUDE AS A TRANSFORMATIVE FORCE

At its core, gratitude is about recognizing and appreciating the goodness in our lives. Gratitude encourages us to shift our focus from what we lack to what we have, fostering a positive outlook that can profoundly impact our mental and emotional well-being. Research in positive psychology suggests that expressing gratitude can improve mental health. Handwritten letters often convey appreciation and gratitude, which can enhance the recipient's mood and overall outlook on life. A study published in the journal ***Emotion*** found that writing letters of gratitude is associated with increased happiness and life satisfaction. When we express gratitude, we engage in a constructive mental process that allows us to savor positive experiences, appreciate the valuable things in our lives, and build resilience against life's challenges.

The simple act of writing a thank-you note encapsulates this transformative power. It forces us to pause, reflect, and articulate our appreciation for someone else's actions, no matter how small. This practice not only makes the recipient feel valued but also reinforces our own sense of gratitude, creating a positive feedback loop that enhances our overall outlook on life. Here are some ways that writing thank-you notes aids you in cultivating gratitude.

1. Allows For a Personal Touch

Handwritten notes create the opportunity for you to make recipients feel valued and appreciated in a way that digital communication cannot duplicate.

2. Bridges Distance

In today's interconnected world, many relationships involve physical distance. Expressing gratitude, especially through a handwritten thank-you note sent by "snail mail," can bridge this gap, making you feel closer to people regardless of geographical barriers. Simple gestures like these remind us that people are an integral part of our lives, despite the miles between us. This is something to be grateful for.

3. Reflects on Gratitude, Mindfulness, and Appreciation

Handwritten thank-you notes show genuine gratitude. As you reflect on the gift, gesture, or effort you have received, you heighten your appreciation for it. This deepens the gratitude you feel and express.

Taking the time to write by hand can also promote mindfulness, reducing stress and increasing focus, which can improve your overall outlook on life and work.

4. Creates a Gratitude Loop, Encouraging Reciprocity

When people feel appreciated, they are more likely to reciprocate kindness and support in the future. When they "pay it forward," it creates a cycle of positivity.

5. Gives You a Professional Edge

Grateful people have higher self-esteem and are more optimistic when approaching problems. They are easier to work with. In a professional setting, handwritten thank-you notes can help build rapport with colleagues, clients, or mentors, showing that you value their contributions or support. People like to work with people they like.

Sending a thoughtful note after a meeting or interview can set you apart from others, reinforcing your interest and leaving a lasting impression that could benefit future opportunities.

6. Enhances Communication Skills

Regularly writing notes allows you to express your thoughts through the lens of gratitude. This increases your emotional intelligence as it enhances your writing skills and improves your ability to express thoughts clearly and concisely.

Writing notes by hand slows down the pace of life and causes you to craft more thoughtful messages—more grateful messages.

7. Creates a Culture of Gratitude

By making thank-you notes a regular practice, you can inspire others to do the same, contributing to a culture of gratitude and appreciation in your community or workplace. As a culture of gratitude is encouraged, this can lead to increased morale and collaboration, benefiting everyone involved.

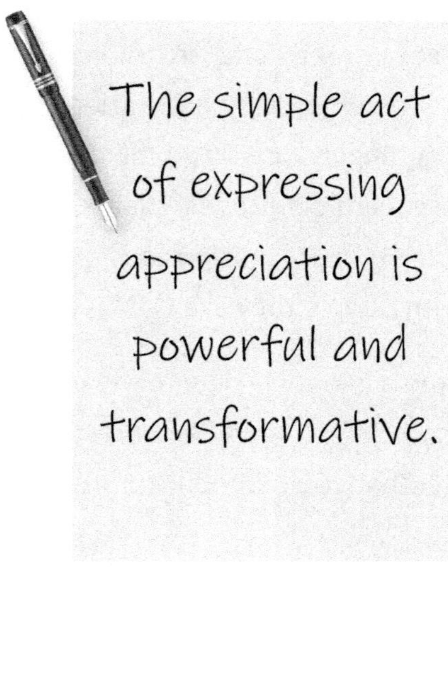

By promoting gratitude, improving communication skills, and fostering a positive culture, handwritten thank you notes can be a transformative force. Do not underestimate the power of the simple act of expressing appreciation.

THE RIPPLE EFFECT OF ACKNOWLEDGING GRATITUDE AND KINDNESS

Gratitude and kindness are contagious. When we express appreciation to others, we inspire them to do the same, creating a ripple effect that can extend far beyond the initial interaction. For instance, when someone receives a heartfelt thank-you note, they are often motivated to pay that kindness forward, whether by expressing gratitude to someone else or by performing acts of kindness themselves. This cycle of acknowledgment fosters a culture of appreciation that can strengthen relationships within families, friendships, workplaces, and communities.

Acknowledging gratitude and kindness through written words can have several ripple effects, including:

1. Enhanced Well-being

Writing about what you are grateful for can boost emotional well-being, increase happiness, and reduce stress. This can promote a more positive outlook on life.

2. Strengthens Bonds

Receiving handwritten letters can enhance personal and family relationships by reinforcing feelings of love, appreciation, and connection. A study published in the ***Journal of Family Psychology*** found that expressions of gratitude, such as those found in handwritten notes, can strengthen relational bonds and increase relationship satisfaction. When people feel appreciated, they are more likely to reciprocate kindness, enhancing social bonds.

3. Increased Empathy

Writing about kindness encourages individuals to reflect on their feelings and the actions of others, promoting empathy and understanding.

4. Encouragement of Positive Behavior

Publicly acknowledging acts of kindness can inspire others to engage in similar behaviors, creating a culture of kindness and gratitude within communities.

5. Improved Communication Skills

Practicing written expressions of gratitude encourages civility and underscores the social contract—things fading in our society. Committing thoughts to paper using ink encourages individuals to articulate their thoughts and feelings more effectively. It is more polite.

6. Creation of a Positive Feedback Loop

When people receive acknowledgment for their kindness, they are often motivated to continue their generous actions, perpetuating a cycle of positivity.

7. Documentation of Positive Experiences

Written expressions of gratitude serve as a record of positive moments, allowing individuals to revisit and reflect on uplifting experiences during challenging times. This fosters resilience.

8. Mental Health Benefits

   Engaging in gratitude journaling or writing letters of appreciation can be therapeutic, helping to alleviate symptoms of anxiety and depression.

9. Encouragement of Mindfulness

   The practice of writing about gratitude encourages mindfulness, as individuals take the time to reflect on the positive aspects of their lives and the kindness they've received.

10. Community Building

    When gratitude is shared publicly (e.g., on social media or community boards), it can build a sense of belonging and community, encouraging collective support and kindness.

Acknowledging gratitude and kindness through written words not only benefits the writer but also creates a positive influence on those around them, fostering a more compassionate and connected society.

Real-Life Story

COLLEGE BASKETBALL COACH WRITES 180 HANDWRITTEN THANK-YOU NOTES EACH MONTH

Buzz Williams, the current men's head basketball coach at the University of Maryland, is widely recognized for his remarkable practice of writing 180 handwritten thank-you notes each month. This commitment reflects his dedication to nurturing strong relationships and expressing gratitude, which he believes helps him remain grounded and focused on his values.

As part of his daily discipline, Coach Williams writes at least two thank-you notes every day, contributing to his impressive monthly total of 180 handwritten notes. This consistent approach ensures that gratitude remains a pivotal part of his routine. The accumulation of these daily notes culminates in writing 180 thank-you notes each month, illustrating his unwavering commitment to this practice.

For Coach Williams, writing thank-you notes is not just a personal habit; it is also an integral aspect of his coaching philosophy. He emphasizes the importance of gratitude and relationship-building, extending this valuable practice to his players. In fact, Coach Williams requires his players to write thank-you notes, teaching them the significance of appreciation and the development of communication skills.

His leadership style and personal discipline demonstrate how handwritten thank-you notes embody his dedication to fostering strong relationships and maintaining a sense of humility and gratitude.

This practice is emblematic of his broader focus on character development and interpersonal skills, for him and his players both on and off the basketball court.

Gratitude Letter Writing Activity

APPRECIATING OTHERS AND CELEBRATING YOURSELF

"Gratitude makes sense of our past,
brings peace for today,
and creates a vision for tomorrow."

MELODY BEATTIE

Expressing gratitude not only deepens our connections with others but also strengthens our sense of self-worth. This activity encourages you to thank someone who has positively influenced your life while also reflecting on your own strengths and accomplishments. Through these heartfelt letters, let's celebrate the kindness we've received and the resilience within ourselves.

Part 1

WRITE A LETTER TO SOMEONE WHO POSITIVELY IMPACTED YOUR LIFE

1. Choose Your Recipient

   Select someone who has made a positive impact on your life. This person could be a colleague, mentor, teacher, coach, family member, or friend.

2. Reflect on Their Impact

   Take a moment to think about how this individual has influenced you. Recall specific instances when they supported you and consider what makes them special.

3. Write and Express Gratitude

   Begin your letter with a warm greeting. Share specific examples of their impact on your life and conclude with sincere thanks. Let your words be heartfelt.

4. Deliver Your Letter

   Send the letter via mail, hand it to them, or read it aloud in person to make the moment more personal and meaningful.

Part 2

WRITE A LETTER TO YOURSELF

1. Reflect on Your Strengths

   Find a quiet place to contemplate your strengths and proudest moments. Think about times when you positively influenced someone else or when you felt proud of your achievements.

2. Celebrate and Acknowledge

   Write a letter to yourself, emphasizing your accomplishments and personal growth. This is your moment to recognize the progress you've made.

3. Conclude with Encouragement

   End your letter on an uplifting note, looking forward to the future. Remind yourself of your potential and express confidence in your ability to continue making a positive difference.

4. Keep Your Letter Safe

   Store your letter in a special place where you can revisit it for motivation when needed. You can also use services like futureme.org to schedule it to be emailed to you on a future date.

CELEBRATING THE BIG AND SMALL

Recognizing and expressing gratitude for both significant milestones and the small, everyday contributions of friends, family, clients, and coworkers is important for several reasons. Celebrating the mundane can add real value to someone's life and foster stronger relationships, enhance well-being, and create a positive environment. Here are some elaborations on why this practice is beneficial:

1. Social Glue

   Gratitude acts as a powerful social glue. Acknowledging the small things—like a coworker helping with a task, a friend listening to a problem, or a family member cooking dinner—demonstrates that you notice and appreciate their contributions. This can deepen bonds and foster a sense of belonging.

2. Happier Environment

Regularly expressing gratitude fosters a culture of appreciation. In workplaces (and in families), this can lead to increased morale, higher satisfaction, and improved teamwork. People tend to feel more motivated and engaged when they know their efforts, no matter how small, are valued.

3. Better Mental Health

Research has shown that practicing gratitude can boost mental health. Acknowledging small acts of kindness can lead to increased feelings of happiness and contentment. It shifts focus from what is lacking to what is present, cultivating a mindset of abundance rather than scarcity.

4. Encouraging Kindness and Reciprocity

When you express gratitude for small things, you encourage the same behavior in others. This can create a ripple effect, where individuals feel compelled to be kinder and more considerate, leading to a more supportive community or workplace.

5. Creating Meaning in Everyday Life

Celebrating small contributions helps highlight the significance of daily interactions and experiences. It adds richness to life by reminding us that joy and appreciation can be found in the routine. This perspective can lead to a more fulfilling life, where people feel valued not just for their achievements but for who they are in everyday moments.

6. Fostering Resilience

Acknowledging the small things can provide a buffer against stress and adversity. When individuals recognize and appreciate the positive aspects of their day-to-day lives, it can help build resilience, helping them cope better with challenges.

7. Building a Habit of Gratitude

Regularly expressing gratitude—whether for big achievements or small acts—can help cultivate a habit. Over time, this can shift one's overall perspective to become more appreciative and mindful, leading to a more positive outlook on life. When you consider these points, it is easy to see that there is just no downside to being grateful, and the benefits will grow like compound interest.

Real-Life Stories

THE "POST-IT-NOTE CAMPAIGN"

KSBJ Radio Station, based in Houston, Texas, has a rich history of serving its community through uplifting music and inspirational messages. Established in 1982, KSBJ has always aimed to provide a positive influence in the lives of its listeners. Over the years, the station has embraced various initiatives to foster community engagement and encourage personal reflection.

One such initiative is the "Post-it Note Campaign," which encourages listeners to express their thoughts, gratitude, prayers, and encouragement on colorful sticky notes. The idea is simple yet profound: by writing down positive messages, individuals can share hope, support, and love with others in their community.

Listeners are invited to write their notes and then either share them on social media using designated hashtags or physically place them in designated areas around the city, such as community boards, coffee shops, or local churches. This grassroots movement not only spreads positivity but also creates a sense of connection among people, reminding everyone that they are not alone in their struggles or joys.

The station often highlights these notes on-air, reading some of the messages to inspire others. During special events and community gatherings, KSBJ sets up "Post-it Note walls" where attendees can contribute their messages, creating a vibrant tapestry of encouragement and gratitude that everyone can see and feel.

Through this initiative, KSBJ reinforces its mission to be a beacon of hope and positivity in Houston. The Post-it Note Campaign has resonated with listeners, reminding them of the power of written words and the importance of community support. By encouraging people to take a moment to write down their thoughts and share them, KSBJ continues to enrich the lives of its audience and foster a supportive environment where everyone can thrive.

THE LETTER THAT CHANGED EVERYTHING

In the quaint town of Maplewood, Minnesota, a bustling community nestled between rolling hills and sprawling fields, lived the Johnson family. At the heart of this family was Emily, a bright, creative sixteen-year-old with dreams of becoming an artist. Her mother, Sarah, was a devoted single parent, working multiple jobs to provide for Emily and ensure she had every opportunity to succeed. Despite the love they shared, the pressures of life had begun to create an unbridgeable chasm between them.

As Emily transitioned into her teenage years, their relationship strained. The late nights Sarah worked often meant Emily was left to fend for herself, culminating in long conversations that rarely took place. Their interactions became increasingly filled with misunderstandings and frustration. Emily, feeling neglected and unheard, retreated into her world of sketches and paintings, while Sarah, exhausted by her responsibilities, often felt her daughter was drifting away from her.

One day, after a particularly heated argument over Emily's declining grades, she stormed up to her room, slamming the door in frustration. As she sat on her bed, tears streaming down her face, she felt a mix of anger and sadness. She loved her mother, but it felt as though they were worlds apart. In a moment of reflection, Emily picked up her sketchbook and began to draw, pouring her emotions onto the page. But instead of feeling better, the weight of the unresolved issues lingered.

After a sleepless night, Emily had an idea. She remembered how her grandmother had always emphasized the importance of heartfelt communication. Inspired, she decided to write a letter to her mother—something more profound than the typical text messages or hurried conversations they had been sharing. She wanted to express her feelings and share her thoughts in a way that would allow her mother to truly understand her struggles.

That evening, while the house was quiet, Emily sat at her desk with a pen and a blank piece of paper. She took a deep breath and began to write:

Dear Mom,

I hope you'll take a moment to read this letter. I know things have been tough between us lately, and I want you to know that I love you more than you can imagine. Sometimes, I feel like I'm in my own world, and I can't find the words to let you in.

I miss you. I miss our talks, our laughter, and just being together. When you're working late, I often feel lonely, like I'm just a shadow in the house. It's hard for me to express how much I need you, but I want you to know that it's not about wanting to complain; it's about wanting to feel connected again.

I see how hard you work for us, and I admire you for it. You're my hero, and I've always looked up to you. But I also want to share my world with you; the art I create, the dreams I have. I want you to be a part of my life, not just as a provider but as my mom, my friend.

Let's find a way to better communicate, not through texts or e-mails. I'd love for us to have some time together where we can really talk. Maybe we can go for a walk or have a movie night? I just want you to know how much you mean to me and how much I want to feel close to you again. I love you!

Love,

Emily

After sealing the letter in an envelope, Emily felt a sense of relief wash over her. She left it on her mother's pillow, hoping that when Sarah returned home, she would take the time to read it.

The next morning, Sarah returned home from her shift and noticed the envelope. Curious, she opened it and began to read. As she absorbed Emily's words, tears filled her eyes. She hadn't realized how distant they had become and how much her daughter longed for connection. The letter struck a chord deep within her, reminding her of the bond they once shared.

That evening, Sarah made a conscious decision to change things. She set aside her work and prepared a simple dinner. When Emily came home from school, she was greeted by the smell of her favorite pasta. Surprised, she walked into the kitchen and saw her mother waiting with a warm smile.

"Hey, kiddo. I got your letter," Sarah said, "can we talk?"

What followed was a heartfelt conversation that lasted hours. They shared their feelings, frustrations, and hopes, bridging the gap that had formed between them. Sarah promised to make more time for Emily, and Emily vowed to communicate more openly about her feelings.

From that day forward, their relationship transformed. They established a weekly ritual of "Mom and Me" nights, where they would catch up over dinner or a movie. Emily began to share her art with Sarah, who encouraged her creativity and even attended her art shows. They laughed together, cried together, and built a deeper understanding of one another.

The handwritten letter became a symbol of their renewed bond, a testament to the power of vulnerability and communication. It was not just a letter; it was a lifeline that changed the trajectory of their relationship forever. Years later, as Emily prepared to leave for art school, she found that same letter tucked away in a box of mementos. With a smile, she recalled how a simple act of writing had reignited their connection and shaped the course of their lives. It served as a reminder that love, though sometimes obscured by the challenges of life, could always be rekindled with a little courage and a heartfelt message.

The power of gratitude is profound and multifaceted. Thank-you notes and expressions of appreciation to close family and close friends are not just polite gestures; they are powerful tools that can transform our relationships and enhance our well-being. By recognizing and celebrating the kindness of others, as well as the small blessings in our daily lives, we can create a culture of appreciation that uplifts everyone involved.

The Power of the Pen

Recognizing and celebrating the small things in life is essential not just for the individuals receiving gratitude but also for building healthier, more connected relationships. Expressing gratitude—whether through handwritten cards, letters, journaling, or gratitude lists—helps us to count our blessings and tap into the strength found in reflection, making us more positive and resilient.

As we commemorate milestones and occasions, our written expressions of gratitude harness the power of positivity and resilience and foster a deeper appreciation for the everyday moments that make life meaningful. By incorporating gratitude into our daily interactions, we contribute to a culture of kindness and connection that enriches both our lives and those of others. So, let us take a moment to appreciate the gifts we have—big and small—and share our gratitude with those around us.

REFLECTION QUESTIONS

These reflection questions are designed to help you internalize the lessons from this chapter and consider practical ways to apply the transformative power of gratitude in your daily life and relationships.

1. Personal Gratitude

   Reflect on a recent moment when someone showed you kindness. How did it make you feel? How could writing a thank-you note to that person enhance the appreciation you feel for their gesture?

2. Daily Acknowledgment

   Think about your daily life. What small blessings do you often overlook? How can you begin a daily gratitude practice to recognize and celebrate these moments?

3. Gratitude in Relationships

Consider the important relationships in your life. How can expressing gratitude strengthen these connections? What specific actions or gestures can you acknowledge in your loved ones through handwritten notes?

4. The Ripple Effect

Reflect on a time when you expressed gratitude to someone. Did it inspire them to share kindness with others? How can you consciously create a ripple effect of gratitude in your community or workplace?

5. Transformative Power

How has practicing gratitude changed your perspective on the challenges you face? What strategies can you implement to maintain a gratitude mindset during difficult times?

6. Weekly Gratitude Practice

Consider implementing a weekly gratitude practice. What specific things would you like to acknowledge about your partner, friends, or family members? How might this practice change your interactions?

7. Mindfulness and Gratitude

How can cultivating a habit of mindfulness enhance your ability to recognize and express gratitude? What techniques, such as journaling or meditation, can help you stay present and appreciative?

8. Overcoming Negativity

Reflect on how negativity can sometimes overshadow gratitude in your life. What steps can you take to shift your focus from negative thoughts to a more grateful mindset?

9. Celebrating Milestones

Think about significant events or milestones in your life that deserve recognition. How can you use gratitude notes to commemorate these moments and strengthen your relationships?

10. Long-Term Impact

How do you envision the practice of gratitude influencing your life over the long term? What legacy do you hope to create through your expressions of appreciation and kindness?

5

CHAPTER FIVE

Special Occasions and Celebrations

"Every life is a story, and every story deserves to be celebrated."

OPRAH

5

Special Occasions and Celebrations

Life is a tapestry of moments woven together by the significant events that shape our journeys. Among these, special occasions and celebrations hold a unique place, marking milestones that deserve recognition and joy. From birthdays to graduations, weddings to promotions, each memorable moment is an opportunity to express our sentiments and convey our heartfelt wishes through handwritten notes and greeting cards. In this chapter, we will explore the importance of these celebrations and the impact of our words in making them truly memorable.

Before we look at the positive ways receiving a greeting card can affect the receiver, let's begin with how greeting cards got their start.

HISTORY AND TRADITION OF GREETING CARDS

Birthdays are perhaps the most personal of celebrations, representing the passage of time and the unique journey of an individual. A simple greeting card for a birthday, holiday, or special occasion with a handwritten note, a thoughtful letter, or a note card can carry a wealth of emotions, reflecting love, friendship, and appreciation. These messages serve as reminders of the joy and significance of life itself.

The tradition of sending greeting cards has a rich history that dates to ancient times. While the exact origins are somewhat unclear, several key developments have shaped the modern practice:

1. Ancient Roots

The concept of celebrating birthdays can be traced back to ancient civilizations, such as the Egyptians, Greeks, and Romans. Originally, only the birthdays of notable people, such as pharaohs or emperors, were celebrated, often with large feasts or lavish parties. The Greeks are often credited with the practice of giving gifts to celebrate birthdays, particularly for children. They would offer cakes to the gods, often shaped like the moon, and celebrate the birthdays of their deities.

The Egyptians sent the first "greetings" on papyrus scrolls as early as 3000 B.C. While this is a far cry from the greeting cards we know today, it shows how long-standing the tradition is.

2. Middle Ages

During the Middle Ages, birthdays were recognized as significant events, particularly among the nobility. However, the practice of sending cards or written messages was not widespread. Instead, celebrations typically involved gatherings and feasting. Those in medieval Europe often celebrated their "name day" on the feast day of the saint they were named after, and it began to take on a more personal nature for the common man.

By the late 1400s, the practice of sending calligraphic messages on parchment decorated with watercolors or even lace can be found.

3. 19th Century

The rise of a middle class and the Industrial Revolution led to more people having the means to celebrate, and the custom of celebrating birthdays became more popular. In the United States, birthday cakes and candles were introduced (hearkening back to the practices of the ancient Greeks). More importantly, the modern custom of sending birthday cards began to take shape. With the advent of the printing press and advances in paper production, greeting cards became more affordable and accessible.

The first known Christmas card was created in 1843 by Sir Henry Cole, a British civil servant, who commissioned artist John Callcott Horsley to design a festive card. This card depicted a family celebrating the holiday and included a message wishing recipients a Merry Christmas and a Happy New Year. Approximately 1,000 copies of this card were printed and sent out, marking the beginning of the Christmas card tradition. Cole is also credited with developing the "Penny Post" system in England, giving rise to the modern postal system by which cards and letters could be sent by people without servants to dispatch the messages. Even Queen Victoria began sending cards, which brought it even more into fashion.

By the 1850s, sending Christmas cards had gained popularity in England, and the practice spread to other parts of the world. The introduction of the postal service and the ability to send cards at a low cost made it even more accessible.

The first known commercial birthday card was produced in the United States in the 1850s. By the late 1800s, birthday cards were increasingly popular, with various designs and messages available for different ages and relationships.

4. 20th Century

By the early 20th century, Christmas cards had become a widespread custom, with various designs, themes, and messages reflecting the spirit of the season.

Joyce Clyde Hall (1891-1982) was the founder of Hallmark Cards, debuting in 1910. He was the first to include envelopes and created cards for occasions throughout the year, and there was a surge in the popularity of greeting cards, including birthday cards. Companies began to produce a wide variety of designs, from humorous to sentimental, catering to diverse tastes. The introduction of mass production made birthday cards even more accessible to the public.

5. 21st Century

More than 3.5 billion people in the United States purchase birthday cards today, with another 1.3 billion sending Christmas cards each year. Data indicates that 6.5 billion greeting cards are sent annually in the United States, with around 90% of households reporting the purchase of at least one greeting card each year.

Perhaps the most telling statistic is that 90% of consumers—even with digital cards, text messages, and DMs—still prefer receiving a physical card to mark occasions. At our core, we crave meaningful, tangible connections, and handwritten messages inside a card do just that.[1]

POSITIVE EFFECTS OF RECEIVING HANDWRITTEN GREETINGS FOR SPECIAL OCCASIONS

1. Creates Shared Experiences

During times of celebration and sorrow alike, a handwritten note conveys effort and thoughtfulness. When you write a thoughtful message to celebrate a milestone, you share in the significance of that experience. The person receiving the card feels celebrated and loved, amplifying the joy of the moment. A card sent for milestones (like retirement or

1 *The History of Greeting Cards* by Michael Q. Bullerdick, posted November 12, 2024 on https://www.harryanddavid.com/articles/holidays/history-of-greeting-cards?srsltid=AfmBOorKrjqp7iT9R_eRmJr6HdNi-wH6ntnhPZ5inrleTotym84JY914z. Retrieved on January 29, 2025.

a new home) can act as a reminder of how far the person has come, inspiring them to embrace the future.

2. Bridges Gaps

An article from ***Thinking Person's Guide to Autism*** by Maxfield Sparrow shared: "Written communication is the great social equalizer. It allowed me to participate and be a part of things bigger than myself." People with autism have difficulty engaging in social situations—particularly large gatherings of family or friends. This makes it more difficult for them to develop social skills that others take for granted, leaving them feeling isolated or ostracized. Writing notes and letters helps bridge that gap and allows them to connect with people they love and who love them. Sparrow went on to say, "Autistic people have valid things to say, and people want to listen with respect if they are helped past our awkward appearance and presentation." Written communication helps with that.

3. Offers Comfort or Encouragement

In times of loss or hardship, a card expressing sympathy or support can provide solace and comfort. It reminds the recipient that they are not alone in their struggles. A heartfelt note can serve as a reminder of the recipient's worth, especially during challenging times when they might feel uncertain about themselves. Handwritten notes can offer words of encouragement and inspiration that motivate the recipient to keep moving forward, especially during transitions or new beginnings.

4. Marks the Occasion

Acknowledging achievements (like a new job or a promotion) can boost the recipient's self-esteem. It reinforces their sense of accomplishment and encourages them to continue pursuing their goals. A card can serve as a tangible reminder of a special occasion. Recipients may keep it as a memento, allowing them to revisit the positive feelings associated with that moment in the future.

Physical cards with photos can be displayed, saved, or cherished, serving as tangible reminders of relationships and shared moments. Recipients can revisit these cards in future seasons, creating a sense of nostalgia and connection.

5. Brings Joy

Receiving unexpected kindness can foster a sense of gratitude. It encourages recipients to recognize the good in their lives and appreciate the people around them. The act of receiving a card can be a delightful surprise, bringing joy and excitement, especially if it arrives unexpectedly. It can brighten someone's day and create a lasting memory. It's special.

As we become increasingly inundated with digital messages, sending physical cards can offer a refreshing break from screens. It's a way to disconnect from technology and engage in the more tactile, personal experience of writing and receiving mail.

6. Establishes Traditions

Regularly sending greeting cards can establish meaningful traditions, reinforce relationships, and share experiences that enhance familial and social bonds.

While digital means of communication are convenient, the tradition of sending greeting cards remains an important and meaningful way to celebrate someone's special day. In essence, sending and receiving greeting cards with handwritten messages fosters a sense of connection, love, and support that can significantly enhance the recipient's emotional well-being. The effort behind a handwritten note goes a long way in making individuals feel cherished and understood, contributing to their overall happiness and sense of belonging.

Real Life Stories

MORE THAN A BIRTHDAY CARD

Clara, from Greenville, South Carolina, was in her late sixties and had been a widow for several years. Her husband, George, had passed away just a few months before their 40th wedding anniversary, leaving a void in her life that she struggled to fill. As her birthday approached, she felt a mix of anticipation and sadness, knowing that this would be her first birthday without him.

On the morning of her birthday, Clara woke up to a too-quiet house. She brewed herself a cup of tea and sat by the window, watching the world outside. The day passed slowly, filled with memories of previous birthdays spent with George, from surprise parties to quiet dinners at their favorite restaurant. As evening fell, Clara felt a wave of loneliness wash over her.

Just then, the doorbell rang. Startled, she got up to answer it, wondering who could be visiting at this hour. When she opened the door, she was greeted by her neighbor, a young girl named Lily, who lived with her single mother down the street. Lily was holding a colorful envelope in her small hands.

"Happy Birthday, Mrs. Clara!" she exclaimed, her face beaming with excitement. "I made you a card!"

Clara felt a rush of warmth as she took the card from Lily. It was decorated with bright drawings of flowers and balloons, and inside, Lily had written a heartfelt message: "You are so special to us! We love you! Hope your birthday is filled with happiness."

Tears welled up in Clara's eyes as she knelt to hug the little girl. "Thank you, sweetie. This means so much to me," she said, her voice trembling with emotion.

Lily, noticing the tears, asked, "Are you okay, Mrs. Clara?"

Clara smiled through her tears. "Yes, darling, I'm okay. You've made my day so much brighter!"

They spent the next hour talking and laughing, with Clara sharing stories of her life as Lily listened intently, her eyes wide with curiosity. Clara felt the loneliness that had weighed her down lift—if only for a moment, replaced by the warmth of connection and the innocent joy of friendship.

As Lily finally waved goodbye and skipped back home, Clara looked down at the card again. It wasn't just a birthday card; it was a reminder that love and kindness can come in unexpected forms. The card was a tangible reminder that even in her solitude, she was not alone.

For the first time in a long while, she felt hope and a sense of community, all thanks to a simple birthday card from a thoughtful little girl.

That small card, filled with crayons and love, reignited a spark within Clara. She decided to host a small gathering for her neighbors, inviting them to share stories and laughter, just as she had with Lily. For the first time in a long while, she felt hope and a sense of community, all thanks to a simple birthday card from a thoughtful little girl.

From that day on, Clara made it a point to celebrate not just her own birthdays, but also the birthdays of those around her, spreading joy and kindness, just as Lily had done for her. In the end, the card was a symbol of a new beginning—a reminder that love, in all its forms, continues to flourish, even in the face of loss.

RITE OF PASSAGE

Graduations mark the culmination of years of hard work and dedication. They represent not just the achievement of academic goals but also the beginning of new adventures. A congratulatory card or note can inspire graduates as they embark on their next chapter, reminding them of their potential and the support of their loved ones. Celebrating this milestone reinforces the importance of education and the personal growth that accompanies it.

For example, Sarah, from Raleigh, North Carolina, was about to graduate from East Carolina University. Like many graduates, Sarah had experienced a mix of excitement and anxiety as the big day approached. Sarah had worked incredibly hard to achieve her degree in psychology, but during her final semester, she faced numerous challenges, including a demanding workload, personal issues, and the pressure of entering the job market.

As graduation day drew closer, Sarah found herself doubting her abilities and questioning her future. She felt overwhelmed and isolated, convinced that her struggles were unique to her. One day, while sorting through some old boxes in her attic, she stumbled upon a handwritten letter from her late grandmother, who had been a significant source of support throughout her life.

In the letter, her grandmother shared her own experiences of hardship and resilience. She wrote about the importance of believing in oneself, even in the face of adversity. "Life may not always unfold as we plan," the letter read, "but every challenge is an opportunity to grow stronger. Remember, you are capable of achieving great things, and I believe in you."

Moved by the heartfelt words, Sarah felt a wave of comfort wash over her. The letter reminded her of the love and encouragement she had received throughout her life. Inspired, she decided to take the letter with her to graduation. On the day of the ceremony, as she walked across the stage to receive her diploma, she held the letter tightly in her hand.

In that moment, Sarah felt her grandmother's presence beside her. The challenges she had faced suddenly seemed less daunting, and she realized that she was not alone in her journey. The memories of her grandmother's unwavering faith in her abilities ignited a spark of confidence within her.

After graduation, Sarah took the lessons she had learned from her grandmother's letter to heart. She began applying for jobs, pushing past her self-doubt, and ultimately landed a position at a local mental health clinic. Her experiences gave her a deeper understanding of resilience, and she often shared her grandmother's story with her clients to encourage them during their own struggles.

Sarah kept the letter framed on her desk. Even years later, it served as a constant reminder of her grandmother's love and the power of words. It served as a symbol of encouragement, reminding her that even in the darkest moments, hope and determination could light the way forward. The handwritten letter not only motivated Sarah during her graduation but also became a guiding force in her life, helping her navigate the challenges and triumphs that lay ahead.

WEDDING GUEST LETTERS

Weddings are one of life's most cherished celebrations, symbolizing the union of two hearts. A heartfelt note or card conveys best wishes for a lifetime of love and happiness. Whether attending the ceremony or sending wishes from afar, these messages contribute to the joyous atmosphere of the occasion, emphasizing the importance of love, commitment, and shared dreams. Weddings are also a time for the bride and groom to thank their wedding guests.

On their wedding day, Tom and Samantha from Katy, Texas, gave handwritten letters of love to each of their 100 wedding guests. They wanted to center their celebration around their closest loved ones and friends—so much so that they wrote a letter by hand to every single member of their wedding party and guests.

"It was a lot of work," Tom admitted, "but it was the most magical moment of our lives."

Samantha echoed his sentiments, saying, "When everyone was reading their letters at the same time, the room was filled with an overwhelming sense of love. Many guests were moved to tears."

Understanding that they might not have the opportunity to speak personally with each guest, Tom and Samantha felt that this was a meaningful way to honor and connect with everyone in attendance. They also took the time to write and mail handwritten letters to those who could not attend their special day.

"The positive love, encouragement, and feedback we received from this gesture will always be a cherished memory from the most special day of our lives," Samantha reflected.

Their heartfelt letters created a lasting bond with their guests, making their wedding celebration truly unforgettable.

Following the wedding, they also wrote and mailed thank-you notes for the wedding gifts they received. Their expression of gratitude reveals their true character and respect for those persons who honored them on their special day.

VIRAL TIKTOK MOMENT

Thomas and Halle are educators from Hope, New Jersey. Their wedding went viral on TikTok for the centerpieces featuring sweet, heartfelt, and funny notes handwritten by Thomas' fourth-grade students in response to two questions: "What is love?" and "Why do people get married?" Among the answers: "When you look at a person, and your heart goes fast, and you're in love" and "So they can get smoochy-smoochy with each other." All of the handwritten notes' images from the centerpieces were compiled into a slide and posted on TikTok. It went viral and amassed over 1.8 million views. This creative gesture was a way to get the children involved with their wedding and form a personal connection with him outside of school while at the same time encouraging the children to handwrite their feelings toward Randle and his new wife to celebrate their special day.

TRANSITION OF POWER

On January 20, 1993, George H.W. Bush (41st President of the United States) wrote a handwritten letter to the newly inaugurated Bill Clinton (42nd President of the United States). The letter is notable for its gracious tone and the spirit of bipartisanship it embodies. The letter's presence in the Oval Office symbolized the peaceful transfer of power and the continuity of leadership in America.

In the letter, Bush demonstrated a gracious acknowledgment of the challenges that come with the presidency. He also emphasized the importance of unity and the continuity of the American democratic process. The letter has since been praised as an example of political civility and respect between political opponents.

The full text of the handwritten letter is often cited in discussions about political decorum and the peaceful transfer of power in the United States.

Below is the transcript of the letter from President Bush to President Clinton.

Dear Bill,

When I walked into this office just now, I felt the same sense of wonder and respect that I felt four years ago. I know you will feel that, too.

I wish you great happiness here. I never felt the loneliness some presidents have described.

There will be very tough times, made even more difficult by criticism you may not think is fair. I'm not a very good one to give advice; but just don't let the critics discourage you or push you off course.

You will be our president when you read this note. I wish you well. I wish your family well.

Your success now is our country's success. I am rooting hard for you.

Good luck,

George[2]

---

2 Note from President George H.W. Bush to President Bill Clinton on https://clinton.presidentiallibraries.us/items/show/101724. Retrieved on January 29, 2025.

MAKING HANDWRITTEN CORRESPONDENCE FOR ALL OCCASIONS A PRIORITY

Matt, the lead pastor of a church in Clayton, North Carolina, has made handwritten correspondence an integral part of his daily life and ministry. As the shepherd of his church staff and congregation, Pastor Matt dedicates several hours each week, scheduled meticulously on his calendar, to personally write handwritten notes and send greeting cards for all occasions throughout the year. These correspondences are directed to his family, staff, volunteers, and first-time guests at his church, each card filled with personal sentiments, scripture verses, and words of encouragement and hope. Additionally, Pastor Matt is intentional about reaching out to fellow pastors across the country with uplifting notes.

By prioritizing personal connections through the thoughtful act of handwritten correspondence, Pastor Matt exemplifies a practice that is often overlooked in today's fast-paced, digital world. His commitment to making people feel valued and connected serves as an inspiring model for both his staff and other pastors, highlighting the significance of personal touch in ministry.

The Power of the Pen

Special occasions and celebrations possess the powerful ability to enrich our lives by offering moments of reflection and emotional expression. By taking the time to acknowledge these significant events through handwritten notes, greeting cards, and letters, we empower ourselves and others to cultivate a deeper sense of connection and joy. Let us embrace the importance of honoring these memorable moments, as they not only create a lasting legacy of warmth and humanity but also remind us of the power we hold in nurturing relationships that endure through time.

REFLECTION QUESTIONS

These reflection questions are designed to help you internalize the lessons from this chapter and consider practical ways to apply the significance of celebrating special occasions through handwritten notes and cards in your own life.

1. Personal Celebrations

    Reflect on a special occasion you recently celebrated, whether it was a birthday, graduation, or another milestone. How did you express your feelings during this event? What role did handwritten notes or cards play in your celebration?

2. Meaningful Messages

    Think about the last time you received a handwritten note for a special occasion. How did it make you feel, and what impact did it have on your perception of the sender? How can you replicate that impact in your own notes?

3. Creating Traditions

    What traditions do you currently have for celebrating special occasions within your family or friend circle? How might you incorporate handwritten notes into these traditions to enhance their significance?

4. Acknowledging Achievements

Consider the professional milestones of your colleagues or friends. How can you make a habit of recognizing their achievements with handwritten notes? What specific messages would you want to convey to uplift and inspire them?

5. Expressing Sympathy

Reflect on a time when you offered or received condolences during a difficult period. How did the handwritten note contribute to the healing process? How can you ensure that you provide comfort in a similar manner in the future?

6. Celebrating New Beginnings

Are there any upcoming transitions in your life or the lives of those around you (new jobs, moves, etc.)? How can you use handwritten notes to acknowledge and support these new beginnings?

7. The Importance of Reflection

How does taking the time to write a note for a special occasion help you reflect on your emotions and relationships? What can you do to make this practice a regular part of your life?

8. Cherishing Small Moments

What small achievements or everyday moments can you begin to celebrate with handwritten notes? How might this practice shift your focus from the big events to the joy found in daily life?

9. Legacy of Connection

What legacy do you want to create through your handwritten notes and celebrations? How do you hope your expressions of gratitude and acknowledgment will impact your relationships over time?

10. Future Intentions

Looking ahead, what specific special occasions do you want to focus on in the coming months? How can you prepare to acknowledge these events meaningfully through handwritten correspondence?

A thoughtfully written letter or note can bridge distances and bring people closer, no matter how far apart they are.

6

CHAPTER SIX

Professional Etiquette in Business

"Think of writing letters and notes as opportunities, not obligations."

DAWN BRYAN

6

Professional Etiquette in Business

Digital communication plays a vital role in today's fast-paced business community. Where would we be without email and instant messaging? However, when the bulk of business communication is digital, the results are impersonal and automated. Handwritten notes and greeting cards can serve as powerful tools to set you apart from your competition. This chapter explores the significance of personal communication in networking, job hunting, and maintaining professional relationships. We will delve into real-life examples of how thoughtful follow-ups and personal touches can lead to job offers and lucrative contracts, and we'll discuss the importance of recognizing clients' milestones to enhance professional connections.

THE POWER OF THE FOLLOW-UP

In the competitive landscape of job hunting and business development, the follow-up is where many candidates and professionals either shine or falter. There is an art to it. Lay it on too thick or seem too eager, and you leave a negative impression. However, a well-crafted handwritten note after an interview or sales presentation can leave a positive and lasting impression. It can keep you top-of-mind as decision-makers weigh their options.

Effective follow-up through handwritten words is crucial for achieving success, whether you are aiming to land a dream job or secure a significant client. Written follow-up serves several essential purposes:

1. Demonstrates Professionalism

   Following up shows that you are organized, committed, and professional. It indicates that you value the relationship and are willing to invest time in maintaining it. In your note, you can highlight key messages or next steps that were discussed during your meeting or presentation, reinforcing your commitment to the partnership. Research has shown that personalized communication can improve customer loyalty and satisfaction.

2. Reinforces Your Interest

   Whether you're applying for a job or pitching a client, a follow-up highlights your enthusiasm and interest. It reminds the recipient of your qualifications or proposal, keeping you top-of-mind in a competitive landscape. It can reference specific moments from your interaction, making it clear that you are genuinely interested in them as a person, not just as a business client.

   You can invite clients to reach out if they have questions or need further information. Handwritten notes can also include a prompt for feedback on the presentation or meeting, showing that you value their opinions and are committed to improving your services. This opens the door for more dialogue and demonstrates your willingness to support them.

3. Expands Communication

Written follow-up provides an opportunity to take the meeting one step further. It allows you to clarify any points discussed in meetings or interviews. It allows you to emphasize and recap key messages, address potential questions, provide additional information, and open the door for a response. It puts a comma after your meeting instead of a period. After a sales presentation, a handwritten note can serve as a memorable follow-up. It allows you to express gratitude for their time and reiterate your enthusiasm for the opportunity to work together.

4. Higher Response Rates

A study by the Direct Marketing Association found that response rates for direct mail campaigns can be significantly higher when handwritten elements are included. Handwritten notes tend to stand out more in a digital world, capturing the recipient's attention. According to a study by the Stanford Graduate School of Business, handwritten notes can increase the likelihood of a positive response from potential customers. The study highlighted that people perceive handwritten communication as more sincere and thoughtful.

5. Builds Rapport and Establishes Customer Loyalty

A report from the American Marketing Association indicated that personalized marketing efforts, including handwritten notes, can lead to higher customer retention rates. Customers appreciate the effort and personal touch, which can make them more likely to continue doing business with a company. Consistent follow-up helps create a personal connection. It is a way to communicate that their time and input mattered to you. People like to help people who appreciate their efforts. No one wants to feel taken for granted. If given the opportunity, people will opt to do business with people they like and trust every time. Building rapport makes you that person.

Handwritten notes give a personal touch and show you are paying attention—genuine caring builds rapport.

Handwritten notes can also be used to celebrate milestones, such as anniversaries or achievements within the client's company, which shows that you're paying attention and care about their success. Genuine caring builds rapport.

6. Demonstrates Proactivity

   Taking the initiative to follow up shows that you are proactive and motivated. This trait is often highly valued in both hiring and client acquisition processes. Against the backdrop of "quiet quitting" and those who do the least they can, demonstrating that you will go the extra mile makes you stand out head and shoulders above the rest.

HANDWRITTEN NOTES VS. DIGITAL FOLLOW-UP

"Well, can't I do all of those things in an email?" you may ask. Sure. In the context of follow-up, both handwritten notes and digital communications each have their strengths, and the choice can significantly impact how you are perceived. There are some distinct advantages to writing a note by hand, however. Let's look at a few.

ADVANTAGES OF HANDWRITTEN NOTES

1. Says Something About You

   An email is easy. It takes little effort to compose and hit send. A handwritten note requires more effort; thus, it is more personal and thoughtful. It says something about your character. A handwritten note conveys that you took the time and effort to express your gratitude or interest, which can create a stronger emotional connection. It suggests that you are willing to go the extra mile.

If you have gone the extra step of having personal stationary or notecards with your name or initials, then you are making an even deeper impression. This level of professionalism and attention to detail becomes part of your personal brand.

2. Makes You Stand Out

In a sea of digital communication, a handwritten note stands out—using handwritten letters can differentiate a business from its competitors. A survey by the United Kingdom's Royal Mail found that 70% of people believe that receiving a handwritten letter is a special experience, which can lead to positive brand perception. In short, it makes you stand out. It is less common, making it more likely to be remembered by the recipient. The tactile nature of a handwritten note can create a sense of warmth and sincerity that may be lacking in digital correspondence.

3. Increased Engagement

Research from the University of Southern California found that handwritten letters have a more significant impact on engagement than digital communication. The tactile nature of handwritten notes can elicit stronger emotional responses from recipients.

ADVANTAGES OF DIGITAL FOLLOW-UP

1. Speed and Efficiency

Digital follow-up is immediate and can reach the recipient almost instantly. This speed can be crucial if the decision to hire or sign is time-sensitive or critical.

2. Ease of Formatting and Editing

There is no spell check or grammar check on a handwritten note. Digital communication allows for easy editing, formatting, and corrections. This may enable you to present information more clearly and concisely.

3. Accessibility

Email messages can be easily forwarded or shared, allowing for broader communication if needed (e.g., forwarding to a team member).

4. Record-Keeping

Digital correspondence can be easily stored and retrieved, making it convenient to keep track of your interactions.

5. The Best Approach

Ultimately, the best approach may be a combination of both handwritten notes and digital follow-ups. Here's a potential strategy:

6. Initial Follow-Up via Email

   After a job interview or client meeting, send a timely email thanking them for their time and reiterating your interest. This ensures you are immediately on their radar.

7. Supplement with a Handwritten Note

   Consider sending a handwritten note timed to arrive a few days later, expressing your appreciation and highlighting a specific point from your conversation. This adds a personal touch and reinforces your enthusiasm. It brings your name back into the conversation.

8. Follow-Up Again Digitally if Necessary

   In the event you haven't received a response after a reasonable period, a respectful digital follow-up can serve to remind them of your interest and keep the dialogue open.

In a competitive landscape, thoughtful follow-up through written communication—whether digital or handwritten—can significantly influence your success in securing a job or landing a client. While digital communication offers speed and efficiency, a handwritten note can distinguish you by adding a personal touch and demonstrating your commitment. The key is to understand your audience and the context, allowing you to tailor your follow-up strategy effectively. Balancing both methods can enhance your professional presence and increase your chances of achieving your goals.

Real-Life Stories

LANDING THE DREAM JOB

Consider the story of Pierce, a sports management professional from College Station, Texas, who interviewed for a coveted position upon graduation with the 12th Man Foundation at Texas A&M University Athletics Department. After each grueling interview, rather than simply sending a generic, impersonal thank-you email, Pierce took the time to write a personalized note to each member of the interview panel. In his notes, he mentioned specific points from their discussions, their backgrounds, and personal lives, and he expressed his enthusiasm for the 12th Man Foundation and the group ticket sales position he was interviewing for. He also sent follow-up e-mails and texts.

The hiring manager later shared that Pierce's thoughtful follow-ups, both "old school" handwritten letters and e-mails after each interview, played a crucial role in their decision-making process. His personal touch not only demonstrated his professionalism but also showcased his genuine interest in the position and passion for Texas A&M and the 12th Man Foundation. Ultimately, Pierce landed the job after four interviews. His genuine and intentional handwritten letters and proactive communication were cited as factors that distinguished him from the other forty candidates.

SECURING A CONTRACT

Take the case of John, from Richmond, Virginia, a freelance graphic designer who pitched a project to a potential client. After the meeting, he sent a handwritten card thanking the client for the opportunity to present his ideas. In the card, John included a brief mention of how excited he was about the potential collaboration and referenced a specific detail from their conversation.

A week later, the client reached out to John not only to express appreciation for his follow-up but also to award him the contract. The client mentioned that John's personal touch and the effort he took to follow up made a significant difference in their decision, as it reinforced the impression that he was genuinely interested in their project.

CELEBRATING MILESTONES GIVES YOU A PROFESSIONAL EDGE

Remembering and acknowledging your business clients' milestones through handwritten correspondence can significantly foster loyalty and strengthen relationships. Here's an elaboration on how this practice can be beneficial:

1. Human Connection

   A handwritten note stands out as a personal and thoughtful gesture. It conveys that you took the time and effort to acknowledge an important moment in their lives. This personal touch can create a deeper emotional connection between you and your clients, making them feel valued and appreciated.

2. Demonstrating Care and Attention

When you remember and celebrate important milestones in your clients' lives, it shows that you care about them as individuals, not just as business transactions. This genuinely fosters trust and rapport. Clients are more likely to remain loyal to a business that recognizes their personal milestones, as it indicates a long-term commitment to the relationship rather than a focus solely on profit.

3. Enhancing Brand Image

A business that prioritizes personal relationships and demonstrates care for its clients' lives can enhance its brand image. This positive perception can lead to word-of-mouth referrals and recommendations as satisfied clients share their experiences with others. A strong reputation for client care can differentiate your business in a competitive market.

4. Creating Memorable Experiences

Handwritten notes for significant life events create memorable experiences for clients. These gestures can leave a lasting impression and make your brand more memorable. Clients are more likely to think of you when they need your services again because you have created a positive association in their minds.

5. Encouraging Client Retention

Loyalty is often linked to emotional engagement. When clients feel emotionally connected to a brand, they are less likely to switch to competitors. By regularly acknowledging milestones, you reinforce this emotional bond and encourage long-term retention, reducing the likelihood of churn.

6. Facilitating Open Communication

Sending handwritten notes can also open the door for further communication. It can prompt clients to respond, share their thoughts, or even provide feedback. This ongoing dialogue can strengthen the relationship and help you stay attuned to their needs, preferences, and changes in their lives.

7. Fostering a Positive Company Culture

Implementing a practice of recognizing clients' milestones can create a positive company culture. Employees who engage in meaningful interactions with clients feel more connected to their roles and the brand's mission, leading to increased employee satisfaction and productivity.

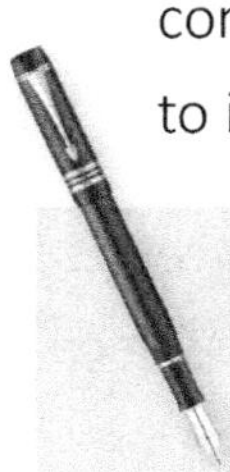

> The handwritten thank-you note isn't just a courtesy. It's a career strategy.
>
> TED JENKINS, FOX NEWS

BEST PRACTICES FOR IMPLEMENTATION

Sending handwritten correspondence to acknowledge your business clients' milestones is a powerful way to foster loyalty, strengthen relationships, and demonstrate that you genuinely care. This thoughtful practice not only enhances client satisfaction but also contributes to long-term business success by maintaining customer relationships and encouraging repeat business.

1. Personalization

   Tailor each note to the specific milestone and the individual. Mention details that are pertinent to them, which shows that you truly remember and care.

2. Timeliness

   Send your correspondence promptly around the time of the milestone. Whether it's a birthday or a promotion, timely recognition reinforces the gesture's significance.

3. Consistency

   Develop a systematic approach to track and remember clients' milestones. This can involve CRM tools or simple spreadsheets to keep track of important dates.

Real-Life Story

THE IMPACT OF RECOGNITION

Ashley, a real estate agent from Raleigh, North Carolina, consistently sends birthday, congratulatory, holiday cards, and other handwritten correspondence throughout the year by mail to her clients. She has seen, over the years, a notable increase in referrals and repeat business. By acknowledging birthdays, holidays, and personal milestones, she not only keeps her name in her clients' minds but also builds a sense of true friendship, family, community, and trust.

Ash's clients feel appreciated and have recommended her services to their friends and family. She consistently wins awards and recognitions for being one of the top real estate agents in the Triangle Area of North Carolina. Every Christmas, Ash also personally delivers pies with a handwritten note to her clients and referral sources. Now that's a personal touch! Ash is consistently recognized as a top performer in the Raleigh-Durham real estate market and attributes her success to the personal touches of written correspondence.

GAINING A COMPETITIVE EDGE

The art of handwritten communication is becoming increasingly rare. However, this scarcity is what makes it so impactful. Taking the time to write a note by hand shows that you value the relationship and are willing to invest effort into maintaining it. It can convey sincerity and thoughtfulness that digital communication often lacks.

In the competitive business landscape, where many professionals are vying for the same opportunities, a handwritten note or greeting card can give you a competitive edge. By integrating this lost art into your professional etiquette, you not only enhance your communication skills but also create lasting impressions that can lead to fruitful partnerships and career advancements.

The Power of the Pen

Professional etiquette in business is about more than just dressing appropriately or adhering to formalities; it's about making genuine connections that have a powerful impact on your professional journey. Handwritten notes, letters, and greeting cards can bridge the gap between professionalism and personal touch, ensuring that you stand out in a crowded marketplace. By following up thoughtfully and celebrating the milestones of those you work with, you create an environment of respect and appreciation that can lead to greater opportunities and enduring relationships, showcasing the true power of meaningful interactions in the professional world.

REFLECTION QUESTIONS

These reflection questions are designed to help you internalize the lessons from this chapter and consider practical ways to apply the principles of professional etiquette through handwritten communication in your career.

1. Personal Follow-Up

   Reflect on a recent professional interaction, such as a job interview or a client meeting. How could a handwritten follow-up note have enhanced your connection with the person involved? What specific points would you want to highlight in your note?

2. Networking Strategy

   Consider your current networking practices. How can you incorporate handwritten notes into your strategy to build and maintain professional relationships? What occasions would be most appropriate for this personal touch?

3. Celebrating Milestones

   Think about the clients or colleagues in your professional network. How can acknowledging their birthdays, anniversaries, or significant achievements through handwritten notes strengthen your relationships? What specific gestures could you implement?

4. Competitive Edge

In what ways do you believe handwritten communication can set you apart in your industry? How can you leverage this unique approach to enhance your professional presence and reputation?

5. Real-Life Application

Reflect on the examples of Pierce, John, and Ashley in this chapter. How did their use of handwritten notes impact their professional outcomes? Can you think of any similar situations in your career where a personal touch could make a difference?

6. Overcoming Hesitation

If you feel hesitant about writing handwritten notes in a professional context, what fears or concerns do you have? How can you address these barriers and embrace the practice more fully?

7. Building a Habit

What steps can you take to make sending handwritten notes a regular part of your professional routine? Consider setting a specific goal, such as writing one note per week or after every important meeting.

8. Reflection on Relationships

How do you currently maintain relationships with clients or colleagues? How might integrating handwritten notes change the dynamics of those relationships and foster deeper connections?

9. Creating a Culture of Appreciation

If you are in a leadership position, how can you encourage your team to embrace handwritten communication as a means of enhancing client relationships? What strategies can you use to model this behavior?

10. Long-Term Impact

Looking ahead, how do you envision the incorporation of handwritten notes affecting your professional journey over time? What legacy do you hope to create through your efforts to connect with others on a more personal level?

CHAPTER SEVEN

7

Crafting the Perfect Handwritten Notes

"A handwritten note can change someone's week—or even their life."

FRANK BLAKE, FORMER CEO OF HOME DEPOT

7

Crafting the Perfect Handwritten Notes

The art of writing a meaningful handwritten note remains a cherished skill. It is a profound way to express emotions, offer appreciation, convey well-wishes, or an apology.

Crafting the perfect handwritten note is not just about putting pen to paper; it requires intentionality and discipline, yet it takes very little time. In this chapter, we will explore practical advice on composing heartfelt messages, selecting the right stationery, and ensuring that your words resonate with the recipient.

PENMANSHIP

In times gone by, penmanship was a skill that was cultivated. Handwriting skills once depicted your social status, education, or profession. Think of the beautiful handwriting of the Declaration of Independence or many historical letters of significance. Whether writing in print or cursive, pride was taken in the quality and clarity of penmanship. There is less emphasis placed on this today, and some people shy away from handwritten notes because they fear their penmanship is lacking and may harm their professional image.

Please do not let your handwriting keep you from composing handwritten notes. Penmanship is a skill that can be developed no matter your age. You can practice dedicated handwritten exercises, slow down your writing pace, and focus on mastering this skill. I promise it will be worth it.

Remember, practice makes permanent. Penmanship is a skill worth cultivating.

TOOLS FOR YOUR CRAFT

Before you begin writing, gather the necessary tools. All you need is a piece of paper, a note card, a greeting card, an ink pen, an envelope, and a postage stamp. Having these items at hand simplifies the process and allows you to focus on the message you want to convey.

1. Paper and Cards

Choose quality stationery that reflects the tone of your message. Whether you opt for personalized stationery, elegant note cards, cheerful greeting cards, or simple pieces of paper, the right choice can enhance the overall impact of your note.

Your choice of stationary or note card is part of your personal brand. It says something about you. Keep in mind that people tend to keep handwritten notes, so choose thoughtfully.

2. Ink Pen

A smooth-writing pen can make a significant difference in how your note looks and feels. Choose a pen that expresses your style, whether it's a classic fountain pen, a sleek gel pen, or one with vibrantly colored ink. Practice writing with a fine-point tip, a medium tip, or a classic nib until you find the pen that makes you feel like your handwriting is confident and strong.

3. Envelopes and Postage

Don't forget to pair your note with an appropriate envelope. A well-sealed envelope adds an air of anticipation for the recipient. My editor's son is from Generation Z—though a young twenty-something, he has become known for his handwritten notes written on parchment, envelopes sealed with wax, and his signature, personalized stamp. This makes him stand out and has opened many doors of opportunity and networking connections.

It is important also to ensure you have the right postage.

4. Technology

Yes, you read that right. Just because you are writing a note by hand does not mean that you can't utilize technology to help you. Whether that is ChatGPT, an online dictionary or thesaurus, or composing the letter in a word processing software first so you can run it through spell-check and grammar check—if these tools make you feel more comfortable and confident in crafting your note—

use them! Once the draft is completed, then write your correspondence by hand. This bridges the gap between digital and analog writing. You'll get the best of both worlds.

COMPOSING HEARTFELT MESSAGES

The heart of a handwritten note lies in the message you convey. Here are some tips for crafting the perfect note:

1. Start with a Personal Greeting

   Begin your note with a warm greeting. Use the recipient's name to create a personal touch. For example, "Dear Emily," or "Hi, John," sets a friendly tone right from the start.

   If the note is more formal, it is appropriate to use their title or position, such as: "Dear Mrs. Smith," or "Dear Mr. President."

2. Express Your Intent

   Clearly state the purpose of your note. Whether you are thanking someone, offering congratulations, or expressing sympathy, being straightforward helps the recipient understand your intent. For instance, "I wanted to take a moment to thank you for your support during my recent project" is direct yet heartfelt. Other examples are: "Thank you for the opportunity to interview with you," "I appreciate the prospect of working with you," and "It was a pleasure speaking with you yesterday."

3. Share Specific Details

Adding specific details and personal anecdotes makes your note more meaningful. Instead of a generic "I appreciate your help," you might say, "Your insights on the presentation not only helped refine my ideas but also boosted my confidence." This personal touch shows that you genuinely value the recipient's contributions.

4. Keep It Genuine

Write from the heart. Authenticity is key in any handwritten note. Your words should reflect your true feelings and sentiments. Avoid overly formal language; instead, let your personality shine through. A casual tone can feel more intimate, especially among friends and close colleagues.

5. Close with Warmth

End your note with a positive message, expressing your wishes or hopes for the future. Phrases like "Looking forward to our next meeting," or "Wishing you all the best in your new venture," leave the recipient with a sense of warmth and anticipation.

6. Sign-Off

Choose an appropriate sign-off that matches the tone of your note. "Sincerely," "Best wishes," "Respectfully," or "With gratitude," are all excellent options. Finally, sign your name with care, as it adds a personal touch to your message.

SELECTING THE RIGHT STATIONERY

Choosing the right stationery can elevate your handwritten note from ordinary to extraordinary. Here are some considerations when selecting paper or cards:

1. Match the Occasion

Use stationery that reflects the occasion. For a formal thank-you note, opt for elegant, understated designs. For a birthday greeting, vibrant colors and playful patterns can enhance the festive spirit.

Keeping a supply of blank note cards on hand is a great way to support the practice of writing notes by hand. With the ability to design and print customized stationery online, there is no reason not to put your signature brand to work for you.

2. Consider the Recipient:

Think about the recipient's personality and preferences. If they have a favorite color or hobby, incorporate that into your choice of stationery. Personalization, in this way, shows thoughtfulness and consideration.

3. Quality Matters

Invest in quality paper and cards. A well-made note card can leave a lasting impression. When you write on quality paper, you will notice the difference in your penmanship. It also signals to the recipient that you took the time and effort to choose something special.

4. The Lost Art of Handwritten Communication

In an era where emails and texts dominate, handwritten notes have become a rare gem. By embracing this art form, you not only enhance your communication skills but also create meaningful connections with others. A handwritten note signifies thoughtfulness, care, and a genuine investment in the relationship.

Handwritten correspondence has seen a decline in popularity due to the rise of digital communication. While older generations may have grown up with the tradition of writing letters, younger generations favor instant messaging, social media, and other digital forms of communication. However, there are several ways to revive the art of handwriting and introduce it to younger individuals in today's digital world.

STRATEGIES TO REVIVE HANDWRITTEN CORRESPONDENCE

1. Educational Programs—

WORKSHOPS: Organize community workshops in schools or libraries where people of all ages can learn the art of letter writing. Focus on the history of handwritten correspondence and its emotional significance.

CURRICULUM INTEGRATION: Encourage schools to include lessons on letter writing in their language arts curriculum. Teach students how to structure a letter, express gratitude, or convey emotions through written words.

PRACTICE: In the workshops and lessons, have students compose and send letters. There is nothing that will underscore the value of this practice like doing it and experiencing the result.

2. 30-Day Letter Writing Challenges—

Create a challenge where participants write a letter each day for a month. This could be themed (e.g., gratitude, friendship) and can be shared on social media to encourage participation.

PEN PAL PROGRAMS: Establish pen pal initiatives where young people can connect with others, both locally and globally, through handwritten letters. This could foster cross-cultural understanding and friendships.

3. Incorporate Technology—

DIGITAL TO HANDWRITTEN TRANSITION: Encourage the use of digital tools to plan letters. For example, students can draft letters on their devices and then transcribe them by hand. This bridges the gap between digital and analog writing.

ONLINE COMMUNITIES: Create online platforms or social media groups and podcasts dedicated to prioritizing handwritten correspondence where people can share tips, ideas, and experiences. Encourage members to post pictures of their letters and discuss their writing process.

4. Use of Social Media—

SHOWCASE HANDWRITTEN NOTES: Use platforms like Instagram and Pinterest to share aesthetically pleasing handwritten notes or letters. Highlight creative calligraphy, beautiful stationery, and the emotional impact of handwritten communication.

HASHTAG CAMPAIGNS: Start a campaign using a specific hashtag (e.g., #WriteItOut, "PowerOfThePen, etc.) to encourage people to post about their handwritten correspondence experiences. This can create a community around the practice.

5. Stationery and Supplies Promotion—

ENCOURAGE STATIONERY USE: Promote the use of beautiful stationery, pens, and other writing supplies. Local shops could offer discounts or themed packages to encourage people to buy and use these products.

DIY STATIONERY KITS: Create and distribute DIY stationery kits that include paper, envelopes, and writing prompts to encourage people to start writing.

6. Create a Culture of Writing to Foster Community—

   Research indicates that receiving handwritten notes can foster a sense of community and belonging, which are important for mental health. A study published in the ***Journal of Community Psychology*** emphasized the importance of community support in promoting mental well-being. Encourage people to write handwritten notes for specific occasions like birthdays, holidays, or thank-you notes. This can be emphasized through social media campaigns or community events.

7. Family Traditions—

   Encourage families to establish traditions around writing letters, such as writing to each other during holidays or special events or maintaining a family journal that gets passed down through generations.

   Make a point to teach children to write thank-you notes, birthday messages, and thoughtful notes to friends and family members.

8. Highlight the Benefit—

   A study conducted by the University of Pennsylvania found that writing letters—whether for oneself or others—can lead to cognitive and emotional benefits, including improved mood and reduced feelings of isolation. This suggests that both writing and receiving handwritten letters can positively impact mental health. Educate young people about these benefits to encourage them to develop this practice.

9. Mindfulness and Reflection—

   Promote handwriting as a form of mindfulness and self-reflection. Handwritten correspondence is sometimes used in therapeutic settings. For example, expressive writing has been shown to have therapeutic benefits for individuals dealing with trauma or emotional distress. Receiving a supportive handwritten note can reinforce the positive effects of such practices. Writing by hand can slow down thoughts and improve mental well-being.

10. Incorporate Art and Creativity—

    ARTFUL WRITING: Combine art with writing by organizing events where participants can decorate their letters with drawings, magazine clippings, stickers, or Washi tape. This adds a creative element that might appeal to younger audiences.

    CALLIGRAPHY CLASSES: Offer classes or online tutorials in calligraphy and beautiful lettering, making the craft visually appealing and engaging.

By employing these strategies, we can help revitalize the practice of handwritten correspondence and instill an appreciation for this art form in younger generations. In a fast-paced digital world, returning to the thoughtful and personal nature of handwritten communication can provide a refreshing counterbalance.

> The practice of writing lowers anxiety as the act of putting pen to paper has a calming, grounding effect.

Studies show that the practice of writing slows the processing of thoughts, lowering anxiety. The act of putting pen to paper is calming—it has a grounding effect. In addition the focus required to write notes by hand and concentrate on the selection of the card or paper, penmanship, and the message provides a comforting distraction that reduces worries and concerns.

Real-Life Story

THE LASTING IMPACT OF A HANDWRITTEN NOTE FROM AN MLB BASEBALL PLAYER

Joey Votto, the talented first baseman for the MLB's Cincinnati Reds Baseball Club, is known not just for his skills on the baseball field but also for his thoughtful nature and unique personality. One delightful story that fans often share involves a handwritten cursive note from Votto that encapsulates his compassion, professionalism, and creativity.

Votto is widely regarded as one of the greatest baseball players to emerge from Canada. For the past 17 years, he has enjoyed a stellar all-star career with the Cincinnati Reds, but as spring training approached this year, he found himself without a team.

In March of 2024, Canadian baseball fans were thrilled to learn that Votto, a Toronto native, had signed a minor-league contract with the Toronto Blue Jays. However, this signing also brought back memories of his controversial comment from 2018, when he stated, "I don't care almost at all about Canadian baseball."

In response to his past remarks, Votto took an unconventional approach by posting a three-page handwritten letter on X (formerly Twitter) to seek forgiveness.

Fans reacted to the letter in two main ways: many expressed appreciation for his apology, while others were amused by his choice to deliver it in cursive handwriting. One commenter humorously noted that the letter was lovely but added, "no one under 30" would be able to read it, highlighting the decline of cursive writing instruction in schools.

Within just 24 hours, Votto's letter garnered significant media attention across Canada and attracted around 1.8 million views from his large following on X/Twitter.

Votto's reflections offer a chance for personal growth and healing, especially given the handwritten nature of the note. In hindsight, he recognized that his careless comments were not only embarrassing for him but also disappointing to his mother. In the letter, he took responsibility for his words and sought forgiveness from those he inadvertently hurt.

"Oof, wow, I cringe and am ashamed as I re-write my words," Votto expressed, acknowledging the impact of his original remarks.

The use of cursive writing added a layer of authenticity to Votto's apology; had he typed it, readers might have suspected that someone else or a computer generated the text. The handwritten note clearly reflects Votto's emotional investment in his apology, complete with some grammatical errors that a typed version would have corrected. While there's speculation that he may have used a "paper tablet," it's unmistakably his handwriting.

For those who appreciate the nuances of handwriting and its significance in conveying meaning, Votto's fully cursive script is particularly interesting. It features numerous connections between letters and is characterized by twists, loops, and backward turns—traits likely influenced by the cursive style he learned during his school years in Toronto.

The Power of the Pen

When you put your pen to paper and compose a handwritten note, you shine. Your handwritten note embodies your essence, expressing your thoughts and emotions in an incredibly personal way. Your handwritten words have the power to encourage and inspire others in a way that no digital communication can ever compare to.

REFLECTION QUESTIONS

These reflection questions are designed to help you internalize the lessons from this chapter and consider practical ways to apply the art of crafting handwritten notes in both your personal and professional life.

1. Personal Style

   Reflect on your preferred style of communication. How does the idea of writing handwritten notes resonate with you? What aspects of your personality can you incorporate into your handwritten messages?

2. Tools and Preparation

   What tools do you currently have for crafting handwritten notes? What stationery items or pens would you like to invest in to enhance your note-writing experience?

3. Purposeful Messaging

   Think about the last handwritten note you received. What made it special? How can you apply those elements to your own notes to ensure your messages are heartfelt and impactful?

4. Specificity and Detail

Consider a recent situation where you expressed gratitude or appreciation. How could you have added specific details or personal anecdotes to make your message more meaningful?

5. Authenticity

How comfortable do you feel writing from the heart? What steps can you take to ensure that your handwritten notes reflect your true feelings and sentiments, avoiding overly formal language?

6. Occasion Awareness

What types of occasions do you typically celebrate with handwritten notes? Are there any upcoming events—birthdays, graduations, or professional milestones—where you could incorporate this practice more deliberately?

7. Recipient Consideration

When selecting stationery, how often do you consider the recipient's personality and preferences? How can you be more mindful about personalizing your stationery choices in the future?

8. Closing with Warmth

Reflect on how you typically end your handwritten notes. Do you feel your sign-offs convey the warmth and positivity you want to express? What phrases could you incorporate to enhance the closing of your notes?

9. Making it a Habit

What specific commitments can you make to incorporate handwritten notes into your routine? Consider setting a goal, such as writing one note per week or after significant interactions.

10. Long-Term Impact

How do you envision the practice of writing handwritten notes affecting your relationships over time? What legacy do you hope to create through your thoughtful communication?

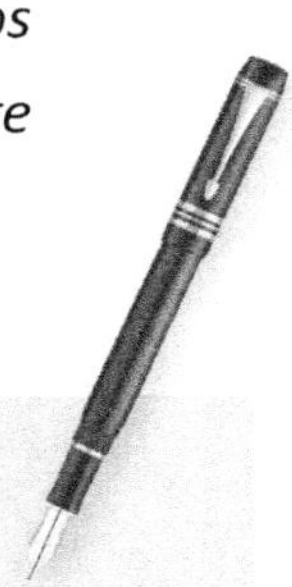

Letters serve as tangible keepsakes that can be cherished and revisited over time.

CHAPTER EIGHT

8

The Lost Art of Letter Writing

"Letters are among the most significant memorials a person can leave behind."

JOHANN WOLFGANG VON GOETHE

8 The Lost Art of Letter Writing

We receive daily instant messages along with social media and email notifications. In that sea of digital communication, the timeless practice of letter writing faces the threat of obsolescence. The rapid evolution of technology has transformed the way we communicate, prioritizing speed and convenience. That has its benefits, but thoughtfulness and depth, sadly, are casualties. This chapter emphasizes the importance of preserving the tradition of letter writing and encourages readers to inspire younger generations to embrace the beauty of handwritten communication.

THE ENDURING POWER OF LETTERS

Handwritten letters have a tangible connection that transcends time and distance. The act of putting pen to paper invites reflection, creativity, and intentionality, creating a space for more profound expressions of thought and feeling. Letters have a unique ability to convey emotions and sentiments in ways that digital communication often cannot replicate.

Kiran Sidhu of *The Guardian* says this: "Emails and texts act like the middleman between the author and the recipient; technology even dictates your words by guessing them and filling them in for you. The pen, however, begs to be enslaved—it needs to belong to you ... When someone sends you a handwritten letter, you receive a part of who they are."

Consider the joy of receiving a handwritten letter in the mail—a delightful surprise amidst the usual bills and advertisements. The tactile experience of unfolding the paper, the uniqueness of the handwriting, and the effort taken to craft a message all contribute to a sense of intimacy that is often missing in a quick text or email. A letter can be a keepsake, a cherished reminder of a moment in time, while digital messages can be easily forgotten or lost in the endless scroll of a device. Handwriting is a skill we need to highlight and encourage. It promotes the flow of thoughts, not just words.

THE TRADITION AT RISK

As technology continues to advance, the art of letter writing risks fading into obscurity. Younger generations who have grown up with smartphones and social media, may not fully appreciate the beauty and significance of a handwritten letter. The convenience of instant communication can overshadow the value of taking the time to thoughtfully compose a message.

Moreover, the skills associated with letter writing, such as penmanship, grammar, and the ability to articulate thoughts on paper, are at risk of being neglected. The educational emphasis on digital literacy often comes at the expense of teaching traditional communication skills, leading to a generation that may struggle to express themselves meaningfully in written form. In many schools, teaching cursive writing has been completely abandoned as archaic, even as research underscores that cursive handwriting improves how the left and right hemispheres of the brain communicate with each other, building neural pathways and increasing mental effectiveness. Iris Hatfield notes, "The ability to master the skill of writing clearly and fluidly improves the student's confidence to communicate freely with the written word. Handwriting is a vital life skill."[1]

INSPIRING THE NEXT GENERATION

To preserve the art of letter writing, it is essential to inspire younger generations to embrace this practice. Here are some ideas for encouraging the next generation to pick up a pen and paper:

1. Share Personal Stories

   Share your own experiences with letter writing—recount the joy of receiving letters from friends or family, or share the excitement of sending a heartfelt note. Personal anecdotes can spark interest and curiosity in younger

1 *"Top 10 Reasons to Learn Cursive" by Iris Hatfield, author of New American Cursive.* © Memoria Press. Posted January 6, 2018. Retrieved at https://www.memoriapress.com/articles/top-10-reasons-to-learn-cursive/ on February 25, 2025.

individuals, making them more inclined to try writing letters themselves.

2. Create Letter Writing Workshops

Organize workshops or community events focused on letter writing. Provide materials such as stationery, pens, and stamps, and guide participants through the process of writing letters. Encourage them to express their thoughts, share their dreams, or even write to historical figures they admire. These workshops can highlight the creativity and fulfillment that comes from the written word.

3. Establish Pen Pal Programs

Connect younger individuals with pen pals, whether they are from different countries, cultures, or even different generations. This exchange can foster curiosity, understanding, and appreciation for the art of letter writing. The excitement of receiving a letter from a new friend can motivate them to engage in the practice regularly.

4. Encourage Gratitude and Reflection

Promote the practice of writing thank-you notes and letters of appreciation. Encourage younger generations to express gratitude for gifts, acts of kindness, or meaningful experiences. This not only reinforces the importance of acknowledging others but also cultivates a habit of thoughtful communication.

5. Lead by Example

Make letter writing a regular practice in your own life. Write letters to friends, family, or colleagues, and share your experiences with others. Your enthusiasm for the craft can inspire those around you to follow suit.

Real-Life Story

CHILDREN EXPRESSING GRATITUDE THROUGH HANDWRITTEN NOTES

Jerry and Kara from Cypress, Texas, have five girls—two in elementary school, one in middle school, and two in college. With so much emphasis on digital communication, they felt it was essential that their girls learn the art of personal connection through handwritten notes. Jerry and Kara routinely encouraged their children to express gratitude and appreciation by handwriting thank you notes, birthday cards, and letters to family and friends. They feel this fosters a deeper understanding of interpersonal relationships. These handwritten notes they work on at the kitchen table together are just not about the words written on the page; they are about taking the time to reflect on what someone has done for them and tangibly expressing their feelings.

This practice cultivates empathy, gratitude, and a sense of responsibility toward others, allowing them to engage authentically in their relationships. Along with handwritten notes, Jerry and Kara also produce personal video messages they text to people to show gratitude.

The personal touch of their girls' handwritten notes stands out in a world flooded with digital communication from children and teens. It shows thoughtfulness and effort. It helps them become intentional in their expression. The girls are learning to slow down, consider their feelings, and articulate their thoughts clearly, nurturing both their writing skills and emotional intelligence. In a society that prioritizes convenience over connection, the Jerry and Kara believe it's vital for their girls to embrace this more genuine and authentic form of communication. They are invested in their girls growing into considerate individuals who understand the impact of kindness and gratitude in their lives and the lives of others.

PRESERVING A TIMELESS TRADITION

The beauty of letter writing lies in its ability to create connections and foster relationships. In a world that often feels disconnected, handwritten letters remind us of our shared humanity. They invite us to slow down, reflect, and communicate with intention and care.

As we stand at the crossroads of tradition and technology, it is essential to preserve the art of letter writing for future generations. By inspiring young people to embrace this practice, we can ensure that the timeless beauty of handwritten communication continues to thrive. Let us celebrate the written word and the connections it nurtures, for in doing so, we honor a tradition that has enriched our lives for centuries.

Real Life Story

TAYLOR SWIFT RESPONDS TO FAN MAIL FOR PERSONAL CONNECTION

There are several instances where Taylor Swift, an American singer, songwriter, and international superstar, has handwritten letters to her fans. These written gestures have had a significant impact on their lives. One notable story involves a fan named Hannah, who shared her experience on social media.

Hannah was dealing with severe anxiety and depression, and she had written a heartfelt letter to Taylor expressing her struggles and how much the singer's music meant to her. To Hannah's surprise, she received a handwritten letter back from Taylor. In the letter, Taylor offered words of encouragement, support, and understanding, which deeply resonated with Hannah.

The impact of this letter was profound. It not only made Hannah feel seen and valued but also provided her with a sense of hope during a difficult time. She described how receiving the letter motivated her to seek help and work towards her mental health. The personal touch of Taylor's response helped Hannah feel less alone in her struggles.

This story, among others, illustrates how Swift's personal connections with her fans can create a positive and lasting impact on their lives, demonstrating the power of kindness and empathy.

The Power of the Pen

The history of handwritten communication reveals its essential role in shaping human connections. From the early civilizations that used symbols to convey meaning to the literary figures who embraced the art of letter writing, the evolution of handwritten communication transcends time and technology. Understanding this history encourages us to appreciate the significance of pen and paper, prompting a revival of the cherished practice of writing handwritten notes and cards.

Writing letters is not merely about words on paper—the power of the pen forges connections, creates memories, and builds a legacy we leave behind. When you pick up your pen and write, you unleash this power and cultivate meaningful communication that transcends time and technology.

REFLECTION QUESTIONS

These reflection questions are designed to help you internalize the lessons from this chapter and consider practical ways to preserve and promote the art of letter writing in your personal and professional life.

1. Personal Connection

    Reflect on a time when you received a handwritten letter. What emotions did it evoke, and how did it differ from receiving a digital message? How can you replicate that experience for others through your own letter writing?

2. Valuing the Craft

    How do you view the significance of letter writing in today's fast-paced, digital world? What aspects of this tradition do you believe are most important to preserve for future generations?

3. Sharing Your Stories

    What personal anecdotes about letter writing can you share with younger individuals to inspire them? How can storytelling about your experiences make the idea of writing letters more appealing?

4. Engaging Others

Consider the idea of creating a letter-writing workshop. What activities or topics would you include to engage participants and help them appreciate the art of letter writing?

5. Pen Pal Program

How might participating in or organizing a pen pal program enrich your life or the lives of younger individuals? What benefits do you think come from exchanging letters with someone from a different background or generation?

6. Gratitude Practice

Reflect on your current practices for expressing gratitude. How could incorporating handwritten thank-you notes or letters of appreciation enhance your relationships and foster a sense of mindfulness?

7. Leading by Example

In what ways can you make letter writing a regular part of your life? What steps can you take to encourage others in your circle to embrace this practice as well?

8. Overcoming Barriers

What challenges do you face when it comes to letter writing? How can you address these challenges to make the practice more accessible and enjoyable for yourself?

9. Legacy of Letter Writing

How do you envision the impact of your handwritten letters on your relationships over time? What legacy do you hope to create through your commitment to this art form?

10. Celebrating Connections

How can you use letter writing to strengthen your existing relationships or build new ones? What specific individuals or groups in your life would benefit from receiving a handwritten note or letter?

Handwritten correspondence
is a timeless tradition that
celebrates the art of personal
connection and communication.

9

CHAPTER NINE

Making Handwriting a Habit

"First we make our habits, then our habits make us."

JOHN DRYDEN

9

Making Handwriting a Habit

Daily habits provide structure and predictability in our lives. They can help us manage our time better, prioritize our tasks, and reduce decision fatigue. Daily habits can significantly influence our mental and emotional health. When we engage in positive habits—whether it's exercising, meditating, or writing—we create a feedback loop that reinforces our commitment to self-improvement. This leads to increased motivation and a sense of control over our lives.

One powerful yet often overlooked daily habit is the practice of creating handwritten letters, notes, or cards. This intentional act of communication is a powerful habit to cultivate. When it aligns with our values and goals, we set ourselves on a path toward success, fulfillment, and happiness.

THE HABIT OF HANDWRITTEN CORRESPONDENCE

It might seem as if handwriting should go on the "endangered species" list of human activities. Technology is so prevalent, easy, and accessible that incorporating handwritten notes into your daily routine may seem like a daunting task. However, the benefits of doing so are great. Writing a handwritten note or card is not a magical feat; it simply requires intentionality, discipline, and a commitment to take the time necessary to express your thoughts on paper.

This chapter provides actionable benefits to both the writer and recipient of handwritten correspondence and shares inspiring real-life examples of individuals who have made writing handwritten notes a regular habit.

BENEFITS FOR THE WRITER

1. Reflection and Mindfulness

Writing a letter requires us to slow down and reflect on our thoughts and feelings. This mindfulness can be therapeutic, offering a moment of introspection amidst the chaos of daily life. Research published in the journal *Emotion* examined the effects of writing gratitude letters. Participants who wrote letters expressing thanks reported increased happiness and life satisfaction. For example, a meta-analysis published in the journal *Psychological Bulletin* found that expressive writing is associated with reductions in symptoms of anxiety and depression. This research implies that a habit of writing letters—especially those focused on gratitude—can contribute positively to one's emotional well-being. Daily writing can have therapeutic benefits.

2. Creativity and Expression

Handwriting allows for creative expression. Choosing the right words, crafting a message, and even selecting the paper and writing instrument can turn the act of writing into an art form. It helps span the bridge between the left and right brain, fostering creativity and encouraging the writer to articulate their thoughts in a more personal manner. Studies such as those cited in *Educational Psychology* highlight that writing by hand, including letters, enhances cognitive processes and memory retention. Regular writing can reinforce learning and improve critical thinking skills.

3. Emotional Connection

The act of writing by hand creates a deeper emotional connection to the message. Articles in social psychology journals have explored how writing letters can strengthen interpersonal relationships. The act of writing personal letters fosters a sense of connection and appreciation, which can lead to increased relational satisfaction. The physical act of putting pen to paper reflects sincerity and thoughtfulness, enriching the emotional weight of the correspondence.

4. Personal Development

Daily writing, whether through letters or journaling, can aid in goal setting and personal reflection. Research published in The *Journal of Applied Psychology* indicates that writing down goals increases one's likelihood of achieving them.

Forbes published an article entitled "How Can Writing Help with Self-Development?" In it, author Dominik Szot writes, "Writing, when embraced as a daily practice, becomes a transformative force for self-improvement, mindfulness, and sharing wisdom. It's a tool to unlock your potential and inspire others." Evidence suggests that a daily habit of writing can contribute to personal growth.

BENEFITS FOR THE RECIPIENT

1. Feeling Valued and Loved

   Receiving a handwritten letter or card is a tangible reminder that someone cares. It uplifts the recipient's spirits, making them feel appreciated and valued in a way that digital communication often fails to convey.

2. Memories and Keepsakes

   Handwritten letters can become cherished keepsakes. Unlike fleeting digital messages, physical letters can be saved and revisited, allowing the recipient to relive the sentiments expressed and the relationship shared.

3. Encouragement and Support

   A thoughtful note provides encouragement during challenging times. It serves as a reminder that the writer is there for the recipient, offering emotional support and reinforcing feelings of connection.

4. Legacy

Letters can be passed down, connecting people to their history. Unfolding a letter written in the hand of one of your ancestors is a powerful thing. It helps ground us to the past and reminds us that we are a participant in a continuing story.

WHY HANDWRITTEN CORRESPONDENCE IS IMPORTANT

Handwritten correspondence serves as a counterbalance to instant messaging and emails, reminding us of the value of personal, purposeful touch. It promotes mindfulness, creativity, and emotional connection—all vital components of healthy relationships.

Handwritten gestures encourage a culture of thoughtfulness and care. They can inspire others to engage in similar practices, creating a ripple effect of kindness and connection within communities.

"On average, Americans receive only four handwritten letters per year."

U.S. POSTAL SERVICE

Real-Life Story

SIMPLE THANK-YOU

Consider the story of John, a busy health care sales and marketing executive from Eau Claire, Wisconsin, who decided to make handwritten notes a part of his daily routine. Initially, he started with simple thank-you notes to colleagues who assisted him on projects. He set a goal of writing at least one note every week. The impact was immediate; his colleagues felt valued and appreciated, resulting in improved team morale and collaboration.

However, the benefits extended beyond his coworkers. John found joy in the act of writing itself. He discovered that taking a few quiet moments to reflect on what he was grateful for helped him cultivate a more positive mindset. Additionally, he received heartfelt responses from those he wrote to, further strengthening his connections and creating a supportive work environment.

STEPS TO MAKE HANDWRITING A HABIT

Making handwriting a regular part of your life requires intentional planning and practice. Here are some actionable steps to help you cultivate this habit:

1. Set Clear Goals

   Begin by setting specific goals for your handwritten notes. Decide how many notes you want to write each week or month. Your goal could be as simple as sending a thank-you note after every meeting or writing a birthday card for friends and family. Having clear objectives will motivate you to prioritize the habit.

2. Establish Designated Writing Times

Identify specific times in your schedule dedicated to writing notes. Perhaps you can set aside 15 minutes in the morning with your coffee or choose a quiet moment in the evening. By establishing a routine, you'll create a space in your day where writing becomes a natural and enjoyable activity.

3. Create a Writing Station

Set up a designated writing area in your home or office where you can keep your stationery, note cards, miscellaneous greeting cards, pens, and envelopes. Having a dedicated space will make it easier to get started and can even inspire creativity. Keep your materials organized and within reach so you're more likely to write when the opportunity arises.

4. Keep a Note List

Maintain a list of people you want to write to or occasions that warrant a handwritten note. This could include birthdays, anniversaries, thank-you notes, or simply a note of encouragement. Having a list will help you stay organized and ensure that no important person or occasion is overlooked.

5. Keep It Short and Sweet

If you're new to writing handwritten notes, begin with short messages. You don't need to write lengthy letters. Sometimes, a few brief sentences are all you need. As you become more comfortable, you can expand your messages and include more personalized details.

6. Seek Inspiration Online

If you want to write more but need a starting point, there's no shortage of inspiration available online. Use Google to find an inspiring quote you can share, or use AI or ChatGPT for specific prompts to help get you going.

7. Reflect on Your Writing

After you write a note, take a moment to reflect on the process. Consider how it felt to express your thoughts on paper and the potential impact on the recipient. This reflection will reinforce the habit and remind you of the joy that comes from connecting with others through writing.

8. Share Your Habit

Encourage friends or family to join you in this journey of handwriting. Share your experiences and the positive changes you've noticed in your relationships. By creating a community around handwritten notes, you can inspire others to embrace the practice as well.

Real Life Stories

TRANSFORMING A CLASSROOM

The benefits of making handwriting a habit extend beyond the act itself. Consider the example of Lisa, a teacher from Cypress, Texas, who began writing notes to her students to acknowledge their achievements and efforts. As her students received these personalized messages, their motivation and self-esteem soared, and their grades drastically improved. This simple practice transformed the classroom environment, fostering a culture of trust and support.

FOOTBALL HELMET NOTES

Todd Durkin from San Diego, California, is a well-known strength and conditioning coach and motivational speaker who has worked with various professional athletes, including those in the NFL. The story of Todd's notes in football helmets revolves around his innovative approach to motivation and mental conditioning for athletes. During his training sessions, Todd would often write motivational messages, key notes, or reminders on sticky notes and place them inside the helmets of the players. This way, when the athletes put on their helmets for practice or games, they would see these messages, reminding them of their goals, the importance of hard work, resilience, and the mental aspects of the game.

This practice was aimed at helping athletes focus on their mindset, reminding them to stay positive and driven, especially during challenging times. The idea was to create a mental edge and reinforce a winning mentality, showcasing how mental preparation is just as critical as physical conditioning in sports. His father did the same for him when he played football. Former New Orleans Saints Quarterback Drew Brees has adopted this tradition as he now places handwritten notes in his son Bowen's helmet prior to his Pop Warner football games.

The Power of The Pen

Incorporating handwritten notes into your daily routine is a powerful practice that can enhance your relationships and enrich your life. By setting goals, establishing designated writing times, and committing to regular practice, you can make handwriting a habit that transforms the way you connect with others. The simple act of writing a note can create lasting memories, foster deeper connections, provide encouragement, and spread kindness in a world that often feels disconnected. Embrace the art of handwritten communication and watch as it becomes a source of joy for both the writer and the reader.

REFLECTION QUESTIONS

These reflection questions are designed to help you internalize the lessons from this chapter and consider practical ways to make handwriting a regular and enriching part of your life.

1. Personal Goals

   What specific goals can you set for yourself regarding handwritten notes? How many notes do you aim to write each week or month? Consider what types of notes (thank-you, encouragement, congratulations) you would like to focus on.

2. Writing Routine

   Identify designated times in your schedule when you can dedicate time to writing notes. What time of day works best for you, and how can you create a routine that makes writing a regular part of your life?

3. Writing Space

   Have you created a designated writing station in your home or office? If not, what steps can you take to set up a space that inspires you to write? What materials will you include to keep it organized and inviting?

4. Note List

Who are the individuals or occasions you want to remember with handwritten notes? Create a list of people or events that warrant your acknowledgment. How will maintaining this list help you stay organized and focused on your writing goals?

5. Starting Small

If you're new to handwritten notes, what short messages can you begin with? Consider simple phrases that convey your thoughts without feeling overwhelming. How can starting small help you build confidence in your writing?

6. Reflecting on Impact

After writing a note, how do you feel about the process? Take a moment to reflect on the emotions you experience when writing and the potential impact your message may have on the recipient. How can this reflection reinforce your new habit?

7. Encouraging Others

How can you share your commitment to handwriting with friends or family? What strategies can you use to encourage them to embrace this practice?

8. Observing the Ripple Effect

Reflect on how your handwritten notes might influence others. Can you think of instances where your notes could uplift someone else or inspire them to express their gratitude? How can this ripple effect enhance your relationships?

9. Personal Benefits

In what ways do you think incorporating handwritten notes into your routine will enhance your own well-being? How does the act of writing help you cultivate mindfulness, gratitude, or connection?

10. Long-Term Commitment

How do you envision the long-term impact of making handwriting a habit in your life? What legacy do you hope to create through your commitment to handwritten communication, both for yourself and for those around you?

Sending a letter can be a therapeutic experience, allowing the writer to reflect and articulate their feelings.

10

CHAPTER TEN

The Digital Dance

"The development of full artificial intelligence could spell the end of the human race."

STEPHEN HAWKING

10

The Digital Dance

Technology permeates every facet of our lives. The pace at which new technology emerges and becomes mainstream is dizzying. Artificial intelligence (AI) stands out among them as a transformative force. From automating mundane tasks to creating art and music, AI has reshaped our understanding of creativity and communication. But even amidst this digital revolution, handwritten correspondence remains resilient and cherished. We can explore and embrace the benefits of AI without undermining the irreplaceable value of handwritten letters, cards, and greetings.

THE EFFICIENCY AND ACCESSIBILITY OF AI

There is no doubt that AI has revolutionized how we communicate, offering remarkable benefits and challenges to our daily lives. The efficiency of AI allows us to draft emails, create to-do lists, summarize meetings, and manage schedules with remarkable speed. Virtual assistants can help us navigate complex tasks, ensuring we stay organized and connected. AI-driven tools can analyze data and generate insights, streamlining communication processes in both personal and professional contexts.

For instance, AI algorithms can suggest responses to messages, predict our needs, and even tailor marketing content to specific audiences. These innovations make communication faster and more efficient, appealing to our increasingly busy lives. As we continue to embrace AI, we find comfort in the convenience it provides, allowing us to engage in dialogue without the burden of time-consuming or cumbersome tasks.

Furthermore, AI has made communication more accessible. Language translation tools break down barriers, enabling individuals from different linguistic backgrounds to connect effortlessly. This democratization of communication fosters understanding and collaboration on a global scale, bridging gaps that once seemed insurmountable.

THE IRREPLACEABLE VALUE OF HANDWRITTEN CORRESPONDENCE

Yet, for all the advantages that AI brings, there exists an intrinsic quality to handwritten correspondence that technology cannot replicate. Handwritten letters, cards, and greetings carry a weight of emotion, thoughtfulness, and personal touch that machines simply cannot emulate.

1. Individuality of Expression

The act of writing by hand is a deeply personal endeavor. Each stroke of the pen reflects the writer's individuality, infusing the message with personality. The varied styles, flourishes, and embellishments reflect the writer's personality and creativity. The imperfections of handwriting (even "sloppy" handwriting brings a smile), the choice of paper or card, and even the ink color contribute to a unique experience. Choosing the right words and adding personal touches transform a simple message into a work of art. This creative expression fosters a sense of individuality that AI-generated messages lack, allowing for a celebration of personal style and expression.

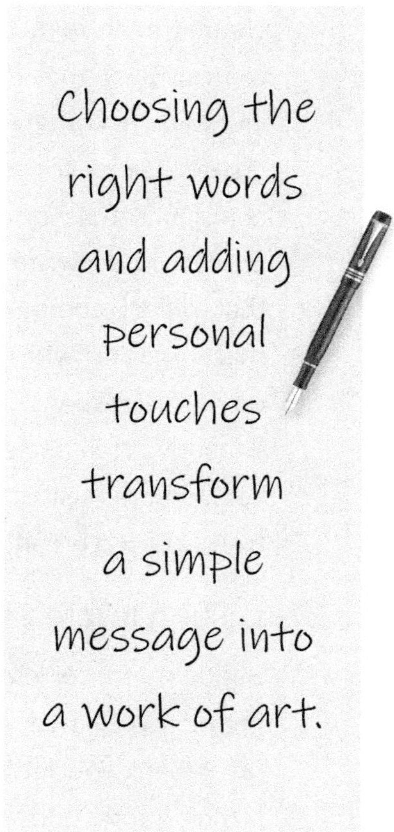

2. Artisan Quality

Head to a bakery. Which would you rather eat—that cheap factory-made, stable-shelf-life, preservative-filled, loaf of mass-produced bread or that artisan quality, created in a time-honored tradition, made from carefully chosen high-quality ingredients loaf? In our fast-paced world, taking the time to write a letter or card demonstrates a commitment to quality. It requires effort, signaling to the recipient that they are valued and worth the time invested in crafting a message. This act of dedication fosters deeper connections, reminding us that meaningful communication often lies in the details. The artisan aspect of handwritten notes provides a tactile experience that digital communication lacks. Studies have shown that engaging with physical objects can evoke different emotional responses. The sensory experience of receiving a handwritten letter can enhance feelings of joy and connection—just like tearing open a warm, crusty loaf of freshly baked bread!

3. Lasting Impressions

Handwritten correspondence has a way of lingering in memory. A birthday card adorned with personal anecdotes or a thank-you letter sharing specific moments creates lasting impressions. These tangible mementos are often kept, treasured, and revisited over the years. In contrast, digital messages soon fade into obscurity, lost amidst the noise of inboxes and notifications.

4. Heartfelt Engagement

The heartfelt engagement when receiving a handwritten letter is profound. The anticipation of opening an envelope, the sight of familiar handwriting, and the sentiment expressed within can evoke a deep sense of joy, nostalgia, or comfort. In times of difficulty, a handwritten note can provide solace, reminding individuals that they are not alone. This emotional resonance is something AI cannot replicate, as it lacks the ability to understand and convey human feelings authentically. AI doesn't know your history or the recipient's story. It cannot tell an inside joke or invoke a distant memory. Only you have that power. Consider a study from the University of California, Los Angeles (UCLA) found that social support is crucial for mental health. Handwritten letters can enhance feelings of social connection and belonging, which are essential for emotional health and heartfelt engagement. The tangible nature of a handwritten note can create a stronger bond than digital communication.

A Real-Life Story

AI & INK

In a small town in Northern California, a quaint stationery and card shop named "Timeless Letters" thrived. The shop's owner, Eleanor, had a passion for handwritten correspondence. She believed that the tactile act of writing brought a personal touch to communication that digital messages often lacked. However, as the world increasingly embraced technology, her business faced challenges. People preferred quick texts and emails over the time-consuming process of writing letters.

One day, while experimenting with an AI writing assistant on her computer, Eleanor had a brilliant idea. What if she could blend the charm of handwritten letters and notes with the efficiency of artificial intelligence? She envisioned a service that would allow customers to dictate their thoughts to an AI, which would then craft the perfect letter for them. The final touch would be Eleanor's own handwriting, transcribing the AI-generated text onto beautiful stationery or greeting cards.

Excited by the concept, Eleanor launched "AI & Ink." Customers would come into her shop, e-mail or text her to share their ideas, and the AI would analyze the sentiment, tone, and purpose of their message. For example, a young man named Jake visited, struggling to express his feelings to a girl he had just met. He spoke about their shared interests and his hopes for a deeper connection. The AI processed his words, creating a heartfelt letter that captured his emotions perfectly.

Eleanor then took the AI's composition and, with her fountain pen gliding over the paper, added the warmth and individuality that only a handwritten note could provide. The final product was a beautiful letter that felt both personal and thoughtful. Jake left the shop with a smile, confident that he could convey his feelings in a way that digital messages simply could not match.

As word spread, "AI & Ink" became a local sensation. People began to see that they could harness the speed and accuracy of AI while retaining the personal touch of handwritten correspondence. Eleanor's innovative approach not only saved the art of letter writing but also created a new form of communication that honored both tradition and technology. In a world dominated by rapid-fire messages, her shop stood as a testament to the beauty of thoughtful communication, proving that even in a digital age, the heart could still find its voice through ink and artificial intelligence.

THE MARRIAGE OF THE DIGITAL AGE AND OLD-WORLD CHARM

A Yellow Letter Writing Campaign is a unique and simple direct mail marketing strategy that employs letters printed on yellow paper. This approach is designed to resemble handwritten notes on a yellow legal pad and plain business envelopes creating a more personal and engaging impression compared to standard marketing materials. Often utilized by real estate investors, this technique aims to connect with potential sellers by appearing less sales-oriented and more approachable.

This campaign is effective for the following reasons:

1. Visual Appeal

The bright yellow color of the letter and handwritten business envelope in red ink stands out in a mailbox, significantly increasing the likelihood that the recipient will open it. The eye-catching hue draws attention and helps the letter to differentiate itself from typical marketing mail.

2. Handwritten Style

These letters are designed to mimic script or cursive handwriting. Using a cursive font gives the impression that the letter was personally written, fostering a sense of intimacy and connection between the sender and the recipient.

3. Targeted Approach

Yellow letters are usually sent to specific individuals based on their property information, which makes the message more relevant and appealing. This targeted approach ensures that the content resonates with the recipient, thereby increasing the effectiveness of the campaign.

HOW TO CREATE A YELLOW LETTER CAMPAIGN

1. Choose the Right Template

Select a template that closely resembles a standard yellow legal pad, ensuring appropriate margins and lines. This attention to detail will enhance the authenticity of the letter.

2. Personalize the Content

Address the recipient by name and tailor the message to their situation. Including details specific to their property can make the letter feel more targeted and relevant.

3. Write in a Conversational Tone

Avoid overly sales-oriented language. Instead, write as if you are having a friendly conversation with the recipient. This approach can help to build rapport and make them feel more comfortable. People like to do business with people they like—so be likable.

4. Include a Clear Call to Action

Be explicit about what you want the recipient to do next, such as contacting you for a free evaluation or consultation. A clear call to action can guide them toward the desired response.

5. Use Tech to Help You

To achieve a high-quality, handwritten look at scale, consider using specialized printing services such as LettrLabs.com. These companies can replicate the appearance of handwritten notes using your own handwriting, ensuring that each letter maintains a personal touch while being produced efficiently. You can design your own or choose from a variety of templates, allowing you to marry technology with the personal touch of handwriting seamlessly.

A yellow letter (or similar) writing campaign is an effective and engaging way to connect with potential clients, particularly in the real estate market. By utilizing visual appeal, a personalized approach, and a conversational tone, businesses can make a memorable impression that encourages recipients to respond.

THE HARMONY OF AI AND HANDWRITTEN CORRESPONDENCE

Rather than viewing AI and handwritten correspondence as opposing forces, we can embrace a harmonious relationship between the two. AI can assist in organizing our thoughts, generating ideas, and even suggesting themes for our letters. It can streamline the logistics of sending messages, but it should never overshadow the beauty of the handwritten word.

As we navigate the digital age, let us remember that while AI offers convenience and efficiency, it cannot replace the soulfulness of handwritten correspondence. The act of putting pen to paper is a timeless ritual that fosters connection, emotion, and creativity. As we continue to embrace technology, let us also cultivate the art of handwritten communication, ensuring that our words remain deeply rooted in the human experience.

In a world where screens often dominate, handwritten letters, cards, and greetings stand as beacons of authenticity, reminding us that some things are simply too precious to be left to algorithms. Embrace both the efficiency of AI and the heartfelt connection of handwritten correspondence, for it is in this balance that we find the true essence of communication in the modern age.

The art of writing by hand is not merely a nostalgic practice; it is a profound expression of our humanity that empowers us to convey our innermost thoughts and feelings. Each letter, card, or note carries with it a piece of the sender's heart and soul, creating lasting memories and fostering genuine relationships. As we embrace the conveniences offered by technology, let us not forget the irreplaceable beauty of putting pen to paper. It is in this harmonious blend of innovation and tradition that we can truly enrich our communication, ensuring that our words resonate with authenticity and warmth in an increasingly automated world.

There is a prevailing duality in our modern communication landscape, where the rapid advancements of artificial intelligence coexist with the timeless value of handwritten correspondence. As we navigate this digital era, it becomes increasingly clear that while AI enhances efficiency and accessibility, it cannot replicate the emotional depth, personal connection, and creativity embedded in handwritten messages.

The Power of the Pen

The power of the pen remains unmatched, serving as a bridge between the technological and the human elements. Ultimately, the challenge lies in recognizing and preserving the power and emotional resonance of our messages, reminding ourselves that the most meaningful connections are nurtured not just through efficiency, but through the thoughtfulness and artistry that only human touch can provide.

As we move forward, let us celebrate both the wonders of AI and the cherished practice of handwritten correspondence, empowering ourselves to find balance in our communication that honors the powerful essence of who we are. In doing so, we embrace the full spectrum of communication—one that is rich, engaging, and deeply human.

REFLECTION QUESTIONS

These reflection questions are designed to help you internalize the lessons from this chapter and consider practical ways to apply the art of crafting handwritten notes in both your personal and professional life.

1. Personal Experience

    How do you feel when you receive a handwritten letter or card? What emotions does this evoke?

2. Value of Time

    In what ways do you think the time and effort invested in writing a handwritten note contribute to the strength of relationships?

3. Creativity and Expression

    How do you express your individuality and creativity when writing by hand? Do you think this aspect of communication is important in today's digital world?

4. AI vs. Handwritten Communication

    Can you identify situations where AI communication is more advantageous than handwritten correspondence? Conversely, are there scenarios where handwritten notes are more impactful?

5. Emotional Connection

How do you believe the emotional resonance of handwritten letters influences interpersonal relationships, especially during challenging times?

6. Technology and Tradition

How can we find a balance between utilizing AI for efficiency and preserving the tradition of handwritten communication? What strategies might help?

7. Cultural Perspectives

Consider the global impact of AI in communication. How does the accessibility offered by AI through translation tools affect cultural exchanges and relationships?

8. Memorability

Why do you think handwritten correspondence tends to be more memorable than digital messages? What role does nostalgia play in this?

9. Artistry in Communication

In what ways do you think the artistry of handwriting enhances the message being conveyed? How does it differ from the impersonal nature of typed text?

10. Future of Communication

As technology continues to evolve, what do you envision as the future of communication? Will handwritten correspondence remain relevant, or will it become a lost art?

A handwritten note can convey sincerity and warmth, strengthening personal connections.

CHAPTER ELEVEN

11

In Their Own Words

REAL-LIFE STORIES OF THE IMPACT OF WRITTEN CORRESPONDENCE

"There's something about a handwritten note that makes it feel more personal and thoughtful than a digital message."

—KATHY KUHL

11

In Their Own Words

As we near the close of our conversation regarding the power of the pen in a digital world, it seems prudent to include social proof. In advertising, particularly in digital marketing, social proof is one of the most powerful tools available. A Neilsen study reported that people largely do not trust crafted advertisements, but their trust factor is much higher when someone else recommends a product or service. In fact, 92% trust recommendations from people they know, and 70% trust consumer opinions posted online from total strangers. Only 36% of people trust ads on social networks.[1]

The reason for this phenomenon is as ancient as the wisdom of Solomon who advised, "Let another man praise you, and not your own mouth."[2] When someone has an experience and shares about it authentically, it gives us the evidence we look for to prove quality and reliability. Testimonials provide real-world evidence. They demonstrate benefits and pitfalls. They prove a concept.

1 Trust in Adversting—Paid, Owned and Earned. © 2012-2025 The Nielson Company LLC. Posted September 2012. Retrieved from https://www.nielsen.com/insights/2012/trust-in-advertising--paid-owned-and-earned/ on March 8, 2025.

2 Proverbs 27:2a, NKJV.

To that end, I wanted to include several real-world stories from actual people written in their own words who have harnessed the power of the pen in the digital age and found its impact to be positive.

Real Life Stories

HOMECOMING PREPARATION

June 10, 2014, would have been my mother's 94th birthday. So, to celebrate her life, I carved out time to go home yesterday and spend the day with my father. I have celebrated her birthday with him every year since she moved to Heaven.

The first few times that I went home after my mother had left, things were not the same. Everything in the house reminded me of her, yet she was not there. Going home almost made my grief more acute. My father must have sensed how I felt, so after a few months, every time I went home, I would find on the kitchen counter a little silver tray with my favorite coffee beans ready for grinding, and my mother's favorite china mug that to this day I love to drink from. In the refrigerator, I would discover my favorite yogurt for breakfast. And when I slipped up to the bedroom I had grown up in as a girl, I would find fresh flowers beside my bed with a handwritten note that said:

Anne,

Welcome Home.

I love you.

Daddy

While I knew one of his sweet caregivers, Amy Morgan, had encouraged him in this and then followed through on his instructions, I still knew I had been expected by my father.

Yesterday was no different. When I walked into the kitchen, although I was only able to spend a few hours with Daddy, my favorite coffee and china mug were laid out on the same silver tray, waiting for me. Since it was a hot day, there was also a beautiful crystal glass with ice and a pitcher of cold tea ready to pour. On the table was my favorite kind of salad and a handwritten note. Once again, I knew I was welcome. I had come home.

Considering how my father prepared for me when he knew I was coming home, I love to think of the preparations the heavenly Father and His Son, our Lord Jesus, are making for my homecoming one day.

ANNE GRAHAM LOTZ
Daughter of Billy Graham
Evangelist and Founder, Angel Ministries
Raleigh, North Carolina

THE PEN SAYS, "I LOVE YOU"

Have you ever heard of The 5 Love Languages *by Gary Chapman? Well, this popular Love Language Test should include a category for handwritten letters—at least for me, this resonates deeply. A written letter is a profound expression of love.*

I have created a bulletin board filled with letters from friends, each a reminder of the thought and care behind the words. Knowing someone took the time to write to me is unforgettable and impacts me in every good way. I have letters that have pulled me through difficult times, like one I received 20 years ago when I was struggling. It was a long letter from someone who cared enough about me to reach out and write to remind me and tell me specific ways I am valued. I keep these letters close to me.

My husband, J.T., has known from our dating days to 34 years later that I treasure letters, and he remains intentional about writing to me. I have kept letters from our time dating to early marriage struggles and reconciliations and sweet surprises he wrote and tucked away in my car, hidden inside my journal and Bible. These notes convey sentiments we might struggle to express verbally; the act of writing allows words to flow in ways that conversations sometimes cannot.

I have always told my kids that my one request for any gift-giving occasion is a long, handwritten letter. I have a collection of these letters, and just thinking about them brings tears to my eyes. They mean the world to me.

In today's fast-paced world, quick and instant communication has its merits, but it lacks the personal touch of a handwritten letter. I grab my phone when I want to go fast and use the least amount of time and thought. It has its benefits. But to hold paper with my dad's handwriting and words is irreplaceable. The letters from J.T. remind me of his love for me from day one, and I will cherish this forever. The words my kids wrote capture moments in time that reassure and encourage me, letting me relive the sweetness of being their mom.

The letters I receive in the mail from friends make me feel noticed and cared about in a heartfelt way that a text will never duplicate.

LISA ECKSTRUM
Cypress, Texas

Simple written thank-you notes of gratitude almost always have a more positive impact than we might have otherwise believed. Theodore Roosevelt said, "People don't care how much you know until they know how much you care." This important saying has lasted for many years because it is so true. I have frequently witnessed its value in both my professional and personal dealings over the past 40 years of my career in two major industries.

My first experience was during my 14 years from 1984 to 1998 as a manufacturer's rep in the primarily blue-collar Industrial Electrical industry. When I began, I had very little training, and most of it was focused on servicing our electrical distributor partners in our channel to our mutual end-user markets of electrical contractors and industrial factories (paper and chemical mills and various manufacturing plants). As was suggested to me by another sales rep in my region, I spent much of my first year taking donuts and sausage biscuits most mornings to the inside sales and counter personnel who worked at the electrical distributors in my territory. This helped me start conversations with my distributor partners, but my sales to those distributors remained flat, and I was expected to grow sales and gain shelf space and conversions to our products.

Christmas arrived about 11 months after I had started my job, and with a small Christmas gift from the company I represented, I included a simple hand-written card to each gift recipient at each of my distributors with a sincere expression of gratitude for their support of our products and their kindness towards me, a very green new sales rep.

When I made my normal "rounds" in early January, I was shocked at how many of the gift recipients went out of their way to tell me how much my hand-written card meant to them! A few also thanked me for the small gift, but I quickly realized that most of my competitors had given the traditional small Christmas gifts to each distributor, so it was nothing new and had become commonplace. I learned that my hand-written note was the differentiator!

My simple hand-written notes had far more impact than anything I had done for those distributors the entire year! Who would have known? My second year was much more productive—distributor partners who had given me very little time or attention my first year took much more time to visit with me each time I stopped by in my second year. Our warm conversations often turned into discussions on how they could convert competitive products to the products I represented! Quite a few of those same distributor partners developed into close personal friends outside of work, and I am convinced that my simple hand-written note of gratitude that first Christmas was the reason. My sales started trending upward in my second year and continued to grow very nicely for the remaining 13 years after! I incorporated the hand-written simple notes of gratitude strategy (to both distributors and end users) for the remainder of my career, and the positive responses I have received have been far more than I would have imagined!

I continued this important practice for the next 26 years, which has been as a manufacturer's rep in the healthcare industry, and similar positive results have continued consistently. I am 100% convinced that simple hand-written notes of gratitude have a tremendous positive impact, and I would encourage any of you in business of any kind to adopt this strategy. I bet you will be very pleasantly surprised with your results!

MIKE FITZGERALD
Drylock Technologies, Regional Sales Director
Memphis, Tennessee

BEING REMEMBERED

When I lost my dad at the age of 17, I lost his words, too. My father was an uplifting person in my life, and knew that my love language was words of affirmation. He never failed to give me daily affirmation. However, a wonderful man, Rod Gray (the author of this book), promised my daddy he would look out for me when he passed. I dubbed that man my "Pops" quickly after my father's passing, and when I went off to college, I was delighted to receive words of affirmation and encouragement from him, too. In fact, between him and my grandfather, the post office ladies on my college campus would ask why I got so much mail! It was all packages and cards from them.

My Pops has never failed to send me cards, Cards to check in, wish me a happy birthday, celebrate a milestone or a holiday, or even when I'm sad. It's like he has a sixth sense to know when I need one of those cards. And I've saved them all, in a bag under my clothes in my closet you'll find cards falling out from how many I have saved. When I moved last October, my friends laughed at how many cards I had jammed in that bag. But when I need an uplifting moment or want to go down memory lane, I simply can just open that bag and look at how loved I am.

Why do I share this? Because we've lost the art of the written word in 2025. As a single woman in her thirties, let me tell you, this generation needs the written word again. I can't get a text back from someone; meanwhile, my grandfather's generation was sending letters while sitting in trenches in the war to their wives, girlfriends, and daughters!

We need the written word. We need the current and next generations to learn a thing or two from those Veterans who wrote all those letters! You see all those cards my Pops sent. And all those care packages my gramps sent to me—they helped heal the grief I felt for losing my daddy. They showed me then and show me now that I am not forgotten. My gramps passed in 2020, and I no longer get care packages from him. But my Pops still to this day sends me cards on the regular—and I love them! I know he sees me, and he's there for me. It solidifies our relationship. Yes, his texts to check in are great. Yes, I love a phone call or a facetime. And I love it when he can visit me in Nashville (hey Pops, I miss you, come visit soon!), but cards show so much love.

He is not just thinking of me but taking into consideration what he knows I like and what is going on in my life. It takes effort to go to a store and pick out a card, write a note, put a stamp on it, and mail it. Written correspondence and the effort behind it is what makes it so special.

So, if you are wondering if it's worth it to send a card, a package, or a note, let me tell you, it is. It heals people in their hardest of times. It shows them you care. It uplifts their spirits. And it makes them remember that they are seen. I hope you will make some effort and send a card to those you love soon—just because you are thinking of them.

ALEXANDRA DETTORE, MSCJ, MA, LPC-MHSP(t)
Franklin, Tennessee

LASTING CONNECTION

For as long as I can remember, receiving and sending cards is something I've treasured in my heart. Maybe it started when I was a little girl, and my mom made it a priority to have my sister, and I make sure to write thank-you letters to our loved ones who took the time to get us gifts. We were taught not just to thank them for the gift but also to let them know one reason we love them. Or maybe it was with my grandmother, who always made it a priority to make sure she never missed a birthday, even up until the day she died at 99 years old. She never once missed sending me a card for my birthday, or my sister, or my cousin, or her great-grandchildren. I once asked my grandma how she remembered our birthdays. She took me into her bedroom to show me a frame of a needlepoint she stitched with all of our birth dates hand-knitted to ensure she never forgot. I think for me, then, the act of receiving and sending cards represents so much more than just the card. It's like for my grandmother, the intentionality of the act. She was intentional to make sure we felt remembered and thought of enough to remember our birthdays. She had to be intentional by taking the time to pick out the card, handwrite a sweet note, put a stamp on it, address it and mail it. It always made me feel so special and loved.

There's also something to be said about a person's own handwriting on a card—both for the person writing the card and for the person receiving the card. With my grandmother not with us anymore, her handwritten cards now mean even more. I miss her so much, but unlike a text that might get accidentally deleted or forgotten, having my grandmother's own handwriting to see with my eyes allows me to feel a little more connected to her. Yes, I do keep my cards! On days when I am feeling nostalgic or a little down, I will pull out my cards and be reminded that someone on the other end thought of me and took the time to let me know something special about myself that sometimes I struggle to see on my own or so easily forget. Handwritten cards feel more personal—they are like a part of someone else is truly being shared with you.

When I give cards to others, I know how much more connected I feel to my own words when I take the time to handwrite a note to someone. Taking the time to handwrite a note to someone else allows me time to sit still with my thoughts and really think about the person I'm sending the card to. I might remember a fun time we've shared together, something I really appreciate about them, or a Bible verse that I'm praying for them. By putting it to pen, I feel more connected to the person I'm writing to, and when we share our gratefulness with others, we are all encouraged! The art of handwriting allows for connection.

LISA THOMAS LPC, CCPT
Cypress, Texas

SPREADING KINDNESS

I began writing as a child when my grandmother started sending letters to me. She lived in Ohio while my family and I were in North Carolina. I was probably around 12 years old at the time, and I looked forward to receiving my own mail so much! We wrote to each other often. This was back in the 1950s when long-distance phone calls were not common at all. My love for correspondence continued when a classmate moved to Florida in the seventh grade, and we began to exchange letters.

Much later in my life, my father came to live with us. He was 92 and had lived in North Carolina since graduating from college, so he had many friends in his second home of Ohio. He loved receiving mail and would rush to the mailbox as soon as it arrived. I started buying him seasonal cards and encouraged him to send them to his friends. This led to his friends sending cards back to him. It was then that I realized how important mail was to both seniors and children.

Since we don't have grandchildren, I enjoy sending cards and letters to some little ones in the hopes that they will appreciate the importance of writing. Two of the families even send me videos of the children opening the cards and letters I send, which I cherish.

When I retired twelve years ago, I increased my card-sending efforts to the shut-in list at our church. I send cards and write notes to them from time to time, aiming to send something monthly.

Our church has started a program where altar flowers that are not taken home by the family are separated and delivered to shut-ins. The wonderful family that initiated this ministry creates a spreadsheet each week with the names of the shut-ins receiving flowers. I write notes to the donors of the original arrangements to let them know where their flowers have gone.

Additionally, we have a program at church that a dear lady started about 25 years ago. We asked the staff at two schools if they would like to have a prayer partner. This partner prays daily and sends them a card each month. When the lady who started the program moved away, I took it over. It brings me joy to see how many people wish to be prayed for and how many parishioners are willing to serve as prayer partners. As you can see, writing letters, notes, and greeting cards is a very important part of my life as I see the impact the written words have in the lives of other people. I hope that through this book, people will be inspired to put down their phones and tablets and pick up a pen to change the lives of others.

SARA FALKNER
Henderson, North Carolina

UNEXPECTED ENCOURAGEMENT

I remember that day so vividly, even now. It was a gray afternoon, the kind where the sky seemed to press down on everything, making it feel heavier than it should. I was stuck in a cycle of despair, the kind that wraps around you like a thick fog, isolating you from everything and everyone. I had been battling with my thoughts for what felt like an eternity, struggling to find a reason to keep going. It was as if I were standing at the edge of a precipice, my heart pounding, teetering on the brink.

Then the mail arrived.

I shuffled to the front door, the familiar creak of the hinges barely registering as I pulled out the small stack of letters and bills. I was about to toss everything aside when something caught my eye—a plain white envelope with my name scrawled across the front in handwriting I recognized instantly. It was from Sarah, my childhood best friend. We hadn't spoken in several years, but the mere sight of her writing sent a jolt of nostalgia through me.

With shaky hands, I tore it open, and as I unfolded the greeting card, I felt that familiar warmth wash over me—as if I were being wrapped in a comforting embrace. The words spilled out like a gentle stream, each one a lifeline thrown to me in my darkest hour:

> Hey Megan,
>
> I was just thinking about you today. I hope you're doing okay. Although we have not communicated in a few years, I felt led by God to send you this card of encouragement, as I know life can get really tough sometimes. I want you to remember how strong you are and that God loves you. You've always been someone who spreads light, even when things seem dark. I believe in you, and I'm here if you ever need to talk. Let's connect on the phone soon. You can reach me at (xxx) xxx xxxx.
>
> Sending you all my love!
>
> Sarah

Tears blurred my vision as I read and reread those simple sentences. I couldn't believe it—she had no idea what I was going through. She was miles away, living her own life, yet her words reached across the distance and found me in my solitude. It was as if she had seen through the fog and reached into my heart, planting a seed of hope where there had been none.

In that moment, something shifted inside me. I felt a flicker of warmth, a reminder that I was not alone, that someone cared enough to reach out despite the years that had passed. I sat down on the floor, the weight of the world still heavy on my shoulders, but somehow, I felt lighter. The note became a beacon, illuminating a path I'd thought had vanished. I realized that I still had a connection to the world—to people who cared, even when it felt unbearable.

That little note didn't solve everything, but it was enough to make me pause, step back from the edge, and know that I was loved by God and He was with me no matter what. It reminded me that life, with all its chaos and heartache, was still worth fighting for. I picked up my phone and sent Sarah a message, thanking her for her words. She replied immediately, surprise and joy spilling from her screen. We began to talk more frequently, sharing our struggles and triumphs and reconnecting in the most beautiful way.

I don't know if Sarah will ever truly understand the impact her note had on me, how it turned the tide when I felt I was drowning. But what I do know is that it was a lifeline I desperately needed, a reminder that even in the darkest times, there is light to be found, and sometimes, it comes from the most unexpected places.

I still cherish this handwritten note today and read it periodically as it is such a reminder I am loved by God and others and to never give up no matter how tough life gets.

MEGAN SMITH
Spring, Texas

WORDS OF LIFE

The dim light of my room felt suffocating as I sat on the edge of my bed, the weight of my despair pressing down on me like a heavy blanket. I had long been battling depression and the grip of substance abuse, and that night, the darkness felt impenetrable. It was as if the world outside had vanished, and I was left alone in a void of hopelessness.

I picked up a pen, my hand trembling, and began to write a suicide note. As the words flowed onto the paper, I laid bare the pain I had carried for so long. I wrote about my feelings of worthlessness, the sense of isolation that had become my constant companion, and how I believed my loved ones would be better off without me. But as I continued to write, something shifted within me. The act of putting my thoughts down seemed to pull me into a deeper reflection.

With each sentence, I started to remember the people who cared about me—my parents, my sister, and my closest friends. I recalled the laughter we once shared, the support they offered during my hardest moments, and the love that seemed so distant now. I realized I was about to leave them with nothing but grief and unanswered questions.

Then, I hesitated.

I thought about the last time my sister had called me, her voice filled with concern and love. I could almost hear her gentle reminders to take care of myself. I paused, pen hovering over the page, and a flicker of something began to grow inside me—a realization that I didn't want my life to end like this. I wanted to fight, to see if there was a way back to the light.

Instead of finishing the note, I turned to a blank page in my journal. I began writing to my family and friends, expressing my love and gratitude for their support, even when I felt unworthy of it. I wrote about my struggles, but also about my desire to seek help. In that moment of vulnerability, I decided that I wanted to be honest with them, to let them in on my pain rather than push them away.

After writing, I picked up my phone and called my sister. I told her everything—the depths of my despair, my struggles with alcohol, and how close I had come to ending it all. Her reaction was immediate and filled with compassion. "You're not alone in this," she said, her voice steady but laced with emotion. "We'll get through it together."

With her encouragement, I sought professional help. Therapy became a lifeline, a safe space where I could unravel the tangled mess of my thoughts and feelings. I started attending support groups, where I found solace in sharing my story with others who understood what I was going through. Writing became a crucial part of my healing process. I filled pages with my thoughts, my fears, and my hopes, allowing the words to flow freely. It was a release, a way to confront the darkness without fear.

Months passed, and while the journey was far from easy, I began to see glimmers of hope. I reconnected with my family and friends, sharing my struggles and victories with them. I wrote them little notes, expressing my gratitude for their unwavering support. Each note felt like a thread weaving me back into the fabric of my life. I learned to celebrate the small victories—waking up without the weight of despair, enjoying a meal with loved ones, or simply taking a walk outside and feeling the warmth of the sun on my skin.

Now, as I sit at my desk, pen in hand and a journal open before me, I can't help but smile. Writing has become my refuge, a way to navigate the complexities of my feelings. I still face challenges, but I have a toolbox filled with coping strategies, and I know I'm not alone in this fight. The suicide note that initially seemed like an end became a catalyst for my rebirth. I am living for the moments that matter, for the love that surrounds me, and for the chance to share my story with others who might be struggling. Each word I write is a reminder that life, with all its ups and downs, is worth living.

And in choosing to write, I chose life.

JESSIE SMITH
Richmond, Virginia

The Power of the Pen

You have just read stories that range from sweet moments of tender nostalgia to gaining the edge in business, to spreading kindness to strangers, to feeling deeply connected and valued, all the way to literally saving someone's life! Each of these testimonials has one thing in common—***they are tied to the power of the pen.*** If I were to edit each of these stories to be about emails, texts, or social media posts, they would fall apart. None of the incredible, meaningful impact you felt as you read their stories would be possible through digital communication. The ink is the lifeblood of the power. The paper is like the joints and marrow, bringing the human element to life and connecting it to others. Handwritten words are intimate. Special.

The pen truly is mightier than the sword. It is powerful because it connects us organically to our humanity—to the authentic, thoughtful expression of our ideas, our values, and our emotions. When we write with our own hand, we connect to centuries of thinkers who put pen to paper before us. Ink is an unbroken thread of history and humanity. The true power of the pen is that it unbridles the power of you. The pen is the tool—you contain the power. Unleash it and watch what happens!

Receiving a card in the mail
can be a delightful surprise
and can convey sentiments
that might be difficult to
express verbally, offering
comfort and support.

12

CHAPTER 12

Pull Out Your Pen

IT'S TIME TO UNLEASH THE POWER

"... nothing will ever replace the sincerity and individualism expressed through the handwritten word."

—DAVID H. BAKER, EXECUTIVE DIRECTOR OF WIMA

12

Pull Out Your Pen

The simple act of sending a handwritten letter, note, or card possesses a remarkable power—the power to change someone's day—or maybe even their life. When we take the time to craft messages of gratitude, encouragement, or love through handwritten communication, we tap into a powerful form of expression that digital messages often fail to convey. Handwritten messages carry a warmth and sincerity that resonate deeply, reminding us of our shared humanity and the profound impact we can have on one another's lives.

Swift texts and impersonal emails dominate our world, but the ink pen emerges as an instrument of influence. The pen empowers the writer to connect in a meaningful way, allowing them to articulate their thoughts and feelings with intention. The very act of putting pen to paper creates a moment of reflection and care, transforming mere words into a mighty message that can uplift, inspire, and comfort the recipient. Each stroke of the pen is a deliberate choice, an investment of time and emotion that digital communication simply cannot replicate.

Imagine the ripple effect of this powerful form of communication—a world where expressions of gratitude, guidance, love, and support are shared more freely. In such a world, people would feel truly seen and appreciated, and relationships would flourish through the simple yet profound act of writing. Creating connections that foster understanding and compassion is the very essence of empowering others through our words.

Now that you have read the testimonials of the powerful pen and learned the incredible benefits that it unlocks, I urge you to commit to reviving the art of handwritten correspondence, recognizing that the world could indeed use a little more kindness, one letter at a time. By making handwriting a habit, we not only enrich our own lives but also inspire others to embrace this powerful form of communication. We have the ability to cultivate a culture of connection and compassion, resonating far beyond the pages of our notes.

TOP TEN TIPS FOR WRITING AUTHENTIC AND EFFECTIVE HANDWRITTEN LETTERS AND NOTES

1. Choose Quality Materials

Writing is more enjoyable when you embrace the ritual of it. Allow handwriting to become a pause from the hurried pace of life. Let it bring you into a place of intentional reflection and gratitude. Select nice stationery or greeting cards that reflect the occasion and your personal style. Quality paper enhances the overall experience of writing a handwritten note, and the one receiving it will appreciate the thought and care that went into choosing the paper or note card.

2. Personalize Your Greeting

When you use the recipient's name in the greeting, you create an immediate personal connection. The choice of your salutation "Dear," "Hi," or "Hello" establishes the tone of the letter. The personal greeting tells the recipient what to expect and makes them receptive to the contents.

Match your tone to the occasion and your relationship with the recipient. A casual tone is appropriate for friends, while a more formal tone may be needed for professional correspondence.

3. Be Genuine and Sincere

Write from the heart. Authenticity matters; express your true feelings, whether it's gratitude, sympathy, congratulations, or just a friendly hello. People know when your words are not congruent with your character or your emotions. When you write with sincerity, you build trust.

4. Specific Details

Include specific anecdotes or details related to your message. Instead of a generic "thank you," say, "Thank you for your help with the project last week; your insights really made a difference." This shows you paid attention and that you value the recipient's contribution.

5. Keep It Simple and Brief

You don't need to write lengthy letters. Even a few heartfelt sentences can have a significant impact. A simple message can convey sincerity and thoughtfulness. Concision contributes to clarity.

6. Reflect on Your Thoughts

Take a moment before writing to think about what you want to express. Reflect on your feelings or any specific memories you want to share. This helps you write more meaningfully.

7. End with Warmth

Close your letter or note with a positive sentiment or well-wishes. Phrases like "Looking forward to hearing from you" or "Wishing you all the best" leave a warm impression. Selecting a sign-off that matches the tone of your message, such as "Sincerely," "Best wishes," "With gratitude," "Respectfully," or simply "Love," communicates your perception of your relationship with the recipient.

8. Add a Personal Touch

Consider adding a small drawing, a favorite quote, or a sticker to your note or the envelope. Personal touches can make your message feel more special and unique.

9. Practice Good Penmanship

In the end, that you wrote the note with your own hand is the most important thing. Some people hesitate to do this because they do not like their handwriting. So practice. It is a skill worth developing. Take your time to write neatly. Clear handwriting enhances readability and shows that you care about your message.

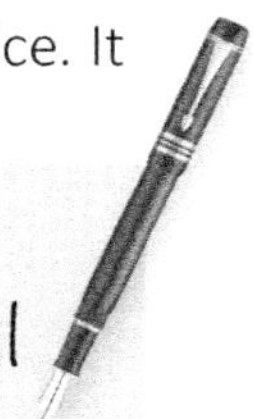

Thoughtful communication strengthens relationships and makes a lasting impact on those who receive your messages.

10. Be Timely

Send your handwritten notes or cards promptly. A thank you card that comes six months after the wedding gift or six weeks after an appointment is discourteous. Timeliness shows that you value the occasion and the recipient's importance in your life.

By following these tips, you can create authentic and effective handwritten letters, notes, and greeting cards that stand out in our digital world. Thoughtful communication strengthens relationships and makes a lasting impact on those who receive your messages.

GETTING STARTED

I have put together a checklist for your handwritten correspondence to help get you started until you create the habit on your own.

1. Gather Your Tools

- Quality stationery (note cards, letterhead, or plain paper)
- Pens (I recommend one that uses smooth-writing blue or black ink)
- Envelopes (matching your stationery)
- Postage stamps (ensure you have the right amount for your letters or cards)

2. Create a Writing Space

- Set up a comfortable and quiet area dedicated to writing.
- Keep your materials organized and within reach.

3. List Recipients

- Create a list of people you want to write to (friends, family, colleagues).
- Include specific occasions (birthdays, thank-you notes, congratulations).

4. Review and Edit

- Once you have written your note, read it aloud to ensure clarity and correctness.
- Check for spelling or grammatical errors.

5. Add a Personal Touch

- Consider adding a small drawing, a favorite quote, or a sticker to make it more special.

6. Seal & Mail

- Place your note in the envelope, seal it securely, and write the recipient's name and address clearly.
- Ensure you have the correct postage.
- Drop it off at the post office or mailbox.

7. Reflect on the Experience

- After writing, take a moment to reflect on how the process made you feel.
- Consider the impact your words may have on the recipient.

8. Make It a Habit

    - Set aside regular time for writing notes and letters, whether weekly, monthly, or during special occasions.
    - Creating a habit ensures that handwritten communication becomes a meaningful part of your life.

APPROPRIATE TIMES TO SEND LETTERS, NOTES, AND GREETING CARDS.

PERSONAL LIFE

1. Thank-You Notes
    - After receiving a gift, attending a party, or receiving help from a friend or family member.
2. Birthday Cards
    - To celebrate friends, family, or colleagues on their special day.
3. Sympathy Cards
    - To express condolences after a loss or during a difficult time for someone.

4. Congratulations Cards

    - For milestones such as graduations, promotions, engagements, weddings, or new homes.

5. Just Because Notes

    - To let someone know you are thinking of them; no special occasion is needed.

6. Get Well Soon Cards

    - To wish someone a speedy recovery from illness or surgery.

7. Holiday Greetings

    - For holidays such as Christmas, Thanksgiving, or New Year's, to spread cheer and connect with loved ones.

8. Anniversary Wishes

    - To celebrate a couple's wedding anniversary or a friend's milestone in their relationship.

9. Encouragement Notes and Letters

    - To uplift someone going through a tough time or facing challenges.

10. Welcome Cards

    - For new neighbors or friends who have recently moved.

BUSINESS LIFE

1. Follow-Up Notes
    - After meetings, interviews, or networking events to express gratitude and reinforce connections.
2. Client, Thank You Notes
    - To thank clients for their business, especially after a successful project or collaboration.
3. Congratulations on Achievements
    - To recognize a colleague's promotion, award, or significant accomplishment.
4. Welcome Aboard Notes
    - For new employees or team members to help them feel welcomed and valued.
5. Client Milestone Cards
    - To acknowledge significant events in a client's business, such as anniversaries or product launches.
6. Networking Follow-Ups
    - After connecting with someone new in your industry, to strengthen your professional relationship.

7. Sympathy Notes for Colleagues

    - To express condolences to a coworker dealing with a loss or personal hardship.

8. Event Invitations

    - For formal invitations to business events, conferences, or corporate gatherings.

9. Holiday Cards

    - To send warm wishes to clients, colleagues, and business partners during the holiday season.

10. Feedback and Appreciation

    - To thank employees for their hard work on a project or to recognize their contributions to the team.

By recognizing these appropriate times to send handwritten letters, note cards, and greeting cards, you can foster deeper connections, express gratitude, and enhance relationships in both your personal and professional life.

Unleash the Power of the Pen

Now is the time to unplug from the busyness of your digital life and dedicate yourself to the transformative experience of putting pen to paper. Let your words flow freely, and watch as they cultivate deeper bonds, bringing joy and comfort to you and the one who receives your letter. Together, we can revive and celebrate the art of connection through the timeless tradition of handwritten notes. We will use ***INK: Discover the Power of the Pen in the Digital World*** to show that the ink pen remains an invaluable tool for fostering genuine relationships and creating lasting impact.

CONCLUSION

Call to Action

"Action is the foundational key to all success."

– PABLO PICASSO

Call to Action

Congratulations! You have finished reading *INK: Discover the Power of the Pen in a Digital World.* As you finish, I urge you to take a moment to reflect on the incredible power that lies within your pen. In an era where genuine connection is often overshadowed by impersonal digital communication, you possess the unique opportunity to bridge the gap and transform your relationships through the art of handwritten correspondence.

EMBRACE THIS CHALLENGE

Commit to writing at least one handwritten note each week- Whether it's a simple thank-you note, a heartfelt letter to a friend, a greeting card for a special occasion, or a note of encouragement to a colleague, each word you pen has the potential to uplift, inspire, and deepen your personal and professional connections with others.

LET YOUR HANDWRITING BECOME A GIFT THAT YOU SHARE

Your handwritten words are a token of your care and thoughtfulness in a world that often rushes past the meaningful interactions we crave. Witness firsthand how a few written words can create ripples of positivity, foster gratitude, and nurture relationships in both your personal and professional life.

RECLAIM THE JOY

Step away from the digital screens, slow down the pace, and reclaim the joy of writing by hand. Your pen is not merely a tool; it is a conduit for human connection, emotion, and legacy. Start today, and together, let us redefine communication in this digital age, one handwritten letter, note, and card at a time.

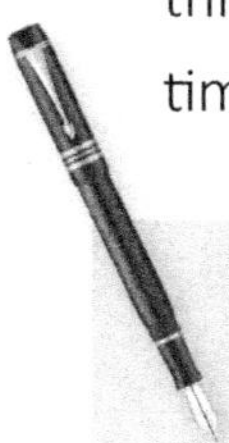

"Act as if what you do makes a difference. It does."

WILLIAM JAMES

TAKE ACTION

Take the Power of the Pen Pledge and let the power of the pen lead you to a more connected and fulfilling life.

Power of the Pen Pledge

As a reader of *INK: Discover the Power of the Pen in a Digital World,* I commit to the following pledge to enhance my personal and professional relationships through the art of handwritten correspondence:

1. Prioritize Connection

   I will recognize the value of personal connections and commit to writing at least one handwritten letter, note, or greeting card each week.

2. Celebrate Milestones

   I will remember and celebrate the special moments in the lives of family, friends, neighbors, etc., by sending greeting cards with handwritten message for birthdays, engagements, weddings, promotions, births, new homes, congratulations, etc.

3. Express Gratitude

   I will take the time to express my appreciation by hand-writing thank-you notes to those who have made a positive impact in my life or done something worth showing gratitude for, no matter how big or small the gesture.

4. Support in Difficult Times

I will extend my compassion by sending handwritten notes or cards to offer comfort and support during challenging times, such as illness or loss.

5. Encourage and Uplift

I will write encouraging notes or cards to family, friends, co-workers, neighbors, teachers, coaches etc., to uplift their spirits and show that I care.

6. Personal Touch

I will make an effort to personalize each piece of correspondence with heartfelt messages that reflect my true feelings.

7. Engage with Community

I will reach out to neighbors, pastors, community leaders, and members through handwritten notes to foster a sense of connection and belonging.

8. Nurture Professional Relationships

I will strengthen my professional network by sending handwritten notes to colleagues, employees, prospective employers, customers, expressing my appreciation, or following up on conversations.

9. Practice Reflection

   I will use writing as a tool for personal reflection, jotting down my thoughts and feelings on paper to deepen my understanding of myself and others.

10. Make Writing a Habit

   I will commit to making handwritten correspondence a regular part of my life, not as a replacement for digital communication, but as a meaningful complement that enriches my connections.

By taking this pledge, I affirm my belief in the "power of the pen" and my dedication to fostering deeper, more meaningful personal and professional relationships through the art of handwritten communication in this digital world.

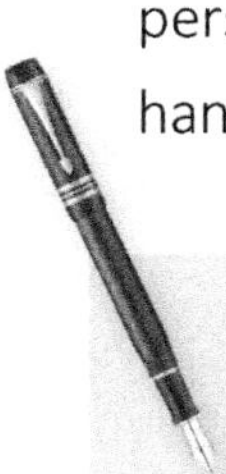

____

Your Signature

____

Date Pledge Made

J O U R N A L

Cultivating Connections through Handwritten Correspondence

"I love those connections that make this big old world feel like a little village."

—GINA BELLMAN

Cultivating Connections Through Handwritten Correspondecne

In this final section, we encourage you to use these journal pages as a tool for reflection and goal-setting in your journey toward meaningful handwritten communication. Building on the insights from *INK: Discover the Power of the Pen in a Digital World,* this space is designed to help you thoughtfully consider the individuals in your life and set tangible goals for reaching out to them through letters, notes, and greeting cards.

1. Reflection on Connections

Take a moment to reflect on the importance of handwritten correspondence in enhancing your personal and professional relationships. What emotions do you associate with writing to others? What impact do you hope your words will have?

---

2. People to Connect With

Create a list of individuals you wish to nurture or improve relationships with. Think about those you've lost touch with or those you'd like to acknowledge.

- Name of Individual:

____

- Relationship: (friend, colleague, family member)

____

- Goal for Connection: (Write a letter, send a note, share a memory)

____

____

____

- Name of Individual:

____

- Relationship: (friend, colleague, family member)

____

- Goal for Connection: (Write a letter, send a note, share a memory)

____

____

____

- Name of Individual:

____

- Relationship: (friend, colleague, family member)

____

- Goal for Connection: (Write a letter, send a note, share a memory)

____

____

____

3. Important Dates and Milestones

- Birthdays: List the birthdays of friends, family, and colleagues to remember and celebrate their special days.

- Anniversaries: Note personal and professional anniversaries that deserve recognition.

- Milestones and Memorable Moments: Record significant life events or accomplishments you want to commemorate, such as graduations, promotions, and special achievements.

4. Goals for Handwritten Correspondence:

Set specific goals for your handwritten correspondence. How many letters or notes do you aim to write each month?

____

What types of messages do you want to convey?

____

____

____

____

____

____

____

____

____

____

____

____

5. Keep This Journal Close

Use this journal to track your progress and reflect on your experiences as you reach out to others. Let it serve as a reminder of the connections you cherish and the relationships you wish to strengthen.

HOLIDAYS TO COMMEMORATE WITH HANDWRITTEN NOTES OR CARDS

The United States is home to a multitude of holidays, both federal and state-specific, as well as cultural, religious, and observance days celebrated by various communities. Here's a detailed list of the most recognized holidays in America, organized by category:

FEDERAL HOLIDAYS

These holidays are recognized by the federal government, and most businesses and schools are closed.

New Year's Day - January 1

Martin Luther King Jr. Day - Third Monday in January

Presidents' Day - Third Monday in February

Memorial Day - Last Monday in May

Independence Day - July 4

Labor Day - First Monday in September

Columbus Day - Second Monday in October
(also recognized as Indigenous Peoples' Day in some areas)

Veterans Day - November 11

Thanksgiving Day - Fourth Thursday in November

Christmas Day - December 25

OBSERVANCES AND CULTURAL HOLIDAYS

These holidays may not be federally recognized but are widely celebrated across various communities.

JANUARY

New Year's Eve - December 31

National Hat Day - January 15

Martin Luther King Jr. Day - Third Monday in January

FEBRUARY

Valentine's Day - February 14

Black History Month - Observed throughout February

MARCH

St. Patrick's Day - March 17

Women's History Month - Observed throughout March

National Pi Day - March 14

APRIL

April Fool's Day - April 1

Easter - Date varies (first Sunday after the first full moon following the vernal equinox)

Earth Day - April 22

National Arbor Day - Last Friday in April

MAY

May Day - May 1

Cinco de Mayo - May 5

Mother's Day - Second Sunday in May

Memorial Day - Last Monday in May

JUNE

Father's Day - Third Sunday in June

Juneteenth - June 19

JULY

Independence Day - July 4

Bastille Day - July 14 (celebrated by French Americans)

AUGUST

National Aviation Day - August 19

SEPTEMBER

Labor Day - First Monday in September

Patriot Day - September 11

National Hispanic Heritage Month - September 15 to October 15

OCTOBER

Columbus Day - Second Monday in October

Halloween - October 31

NOVEMBER

Veterans Day - November 11

Thanksgiving Day - Fourth Thursday in November

Black Friday - Day after Thanksgiving

Cyber Monday - Monday after Thanksgiving

DECEMBER

Hanukkah - Date varies (usually falls in December)

Christmas Eve - December 24

Christmas Day - December 25

Kwanzaa - December 26 to January 1

New Year's Eve - December 31

RELIGIOUS HOLIDAYS

In addition to the holidays listed above, various religious groups observe their own holidays. Some of these may overlap with the secular calendar.

Ramadan - Date varies (Islamic lunar calendar)

Eid al-Fitr - Date varies (Islamic lunar calendar)

Eid al-Adha - Date varies (Islamic lunar calendar)

Diwali - Date varies (Hindu festival of lights)

Buddha's Birthday - Date varies (observed by Buddhists)

Ash Wednesday - Date varies (Christian observance)

Lent - Date varies (Christian observance leading up to Easter)

REGIONAL AND STATE HOLIDAYS

Certain holidays are celebrated regionally or within specific states. Examples include:

Mardi Gras - Celebrated in New Orleans and parts of the Gulf Coast (around February/March)

Patriot's Day - Celebrated in Massachusetts and Maine on the third Monday in April

California Admission Day - September 9 in California

Texas Independence Day - March 2 in Texas

CONCLUSION

This list covers many of the significant holidays celebrated in the United States, though regional variations and personal observances can lead to additional celebrations. The diversity of the American population means that many more holidays are observed within specific communities, reflecting the rich cultural tapestry of the nation.

About the Author

Rod Gray is a seasoned professional with over 30 years of experience in medical sales, sales management, and executive leadership within both the corporate and nonprofit sectors. Throughout his award-winning career, he has exemplified servant leadership by prioritizing relationship-building and fostering meaningful connections in all aspects of his personal and professional life.

Rod practices gratitude and compassion daily, particularly through the art of written correspondence. He harnesses the power of the pen to positively impact both his life and the lives of others.

In INK: Discover the Power of the Pen in a Digital World, Rod explores the profound impact of genuine, handwritten correspondence in our increasingly digital landscape. His insights emphasize the significance of authentic connections and highlight the written word's ability to bridge distances and strengthen relationships. His commitment to fostering connections extends to his involvement in community service and nonprofit organizations, as well as his active participation in his local church.

Passionate about embodying the core values he espouses, Rod inspires others to embrace and discover the joy of personal written correspondence and experience the transformative power of the ink pen in a digital age. His journey serves as a testament to the enduring strength of words and the heartfelt intention behind every message.

When not writing or working, Rod enjoys spending quality time with his family and friends and is an avid sports enthusiast. He resides in Cypress, Texas, with his wife of 30 years, Amie. Together, they have two adult children, Owen Gray and Olivia Bradley, who inspire him daily.

Connect With Rod and Share Your Stories

INKPOWEROFTHEPEN.COM

EMAIL: rod@inkpowerofthepen.com

SOCIAL MEDIA:

FACEBOOK: Rod Gray

INSTAGRAM: @rodgray00

X (FORMERLY TWITTER): @rodgray

LINKEDIN: Rod Gray

Printed in Dunstable, United Kingdom

79649526R00157